LONDON ARCHITECTURE

LONDON ARCHITECTURE

FKG

F K G

Editorial project:
2010 © LOFT Publications
Via Laietana, 32, 4.º, Of. 92
08003 Barcelona, Spain
Tel.: +34 932 688 088
Fax: +34 932 687 073
loft@loftpublications.com
www.loftpublications.com

Created and distributed in cooperation with Frechmann Kolón GmbH
www.frechmann.com

Editor:
Daniela Santos Quartino

Editorial coordinator:
Simone K. Schleifer

Assistant to editorial coordination:
Aitana Lleonart

Art director:
Mireia Casanovas Soley

Design and layout coordination:
Claudia Martínez Alonso

Cover layout:
Nacho Gràcia Blanco

Layout:
Cristina Simó Perales, Yolanda G. Román

Translations:
Equipo de Edición

ISBN:
978-84-92731-08-4 (INT)
978-80-556-0009-3 (SLOVART)

Printed in China

Cover photo:
Patrick Petruchelli

If you would like to propose works to include in our upcoming books, please email us at loft@loftpublications.com.

In some cases it has been impossible to locate copyright owners of the images published in this book. Please contact the publisher if you are the copyright owner of any of the images published here.

Westminster Abbey, Houses of Parliament (with the Big Ben clock tower) and Tower Bridge are no longer the only reference buildings in the city of London. Its English Gothic outline today competes with the daring lines and groundbreaking forms of the contemporary architecture being raised every day in the capital of the United Kingdom.

The Swiss Re building known as the Gherkin, the huge London Eye ferris wheel, the Millennium Bridge, the O2 Arena and the futuristic buildings of Canary Wharf are among the landmarks of a city that confidently boasts a mix of tradition and future.

This volume is a visual guide to the transformations that have taken place in the city in recent years. It also covers the classical buildings of unquestionable architectural quality that have helped form the character of one of the most vibrant cities on Earth.

Westminster Abbey, das Parlamentsgebäude mit dem Big Ben und die Tower Bridge sind längst nicht mehr die einzigen weltweit bekannten Bauwerke Londons. Die grazilen Türme der englischen Gotik müssen sich heute neben den gewagten Linien und neuartigen Formen der zeitgenössischen Architektur behaupten, die in der britischen Hauptstadt in unablässiger Folge neu entstehen.

Das Gebäude der Swiss Re, wegen seiner ungewöhnlichen Form auch als „Gurke" bekannt, das riesenhafte London Eye, die Millenium Bridge, die O2 Arena oder die futuristischen Gebäude der Canary Wharf gehören mittlerweile zu den Wahrzeichen einer Stadt, die sich ohne Komplexe zwischen Tradition und Zukunft bewegt.

Anhand der Aufnahmen im vorliegenden Band lassen sich die Veränderungen der britischen Hauptstadt in den letzten Jahren anschaulich nachvollziehen. Dabei werden auch die anderen Bauwerke nicht vergessen, die aufgrund ihrer architektonischen Qualität unzweifelhaft mit dazu beigetragen haben, London zu einer der aufregendsten Städte der Welt zu machen.

L'Abbaye de Westminster, les Houses of Parliament (et la tour de Big Ben) et le Tower Bridge ne sont plus les seuls bâtiments de référence de Londres. Leurs silhouettes moulées par le gothique anglais côtoient aujourd'hui les lignes osées et les formes innovantes de l'architecture contemporaine qui voit le jour dans la capitale du Royaume-Uni.

À l'heure actuelle, le bâtiment Swiss Re, connue comme le Gherkin pour sa forme de cornichon, l'énorme roue du London Eye, le pont du Millenium ou l'enceinte O2 Arena, ainsi que les constructions futuristes de Canary Wharf, s'inscrivent comment points de repère d'une ville qui se balance sans complexes entre tradition et futur.

Le présent ouvrage offre un guide visuel des transformations s'étant produites à Londres au cours des dernières années. Il n'oublie pas les bâtiments classiques d'une qualité architectonique indiscutable ayant contribué à forger le caractère de l'une des villes les plus émouvantes de la planète.

Westminster Abbey, de Houses of Parliament (met de Big Ben) en de Tower Bridge zijn niet langer de enige bouwwerken die Londen karakteriseren. Deze door de Engelse gotiek gevormde silhouetten delen hun hoofdrol tegenwoordig met de gedurfde lijnen en innoverende vormen van de hedendaagse architectuur, waar onafgebroken aan gebouwd wordt in de hoofdstad van het Verenigd Koninkrijk.

Tegenwoordig staan ook het gebouw van Swiss Re, dat vanwege zijn augurkvorm The Gerkin wordt genoemd, het gigantische reuzenrad London Eye, de Millennium Bridge, de O2 arena en zelfs de futuristische gebouwen van Canary Wharf op de ansichtkaarten van Londen, een stad die zich moeiteloos tussen traditie en toekomst beweegt.

Dit boek laat als een beeldgids zien welke veranderingen zich de laatste jaren in deze stad hebben voorgedaan. Maar het gaat niet voorbij aan de klassieke gebouwen die onomstotelijk van architectonische waarde zijn en mede het karakter van een van de bruisendste steden op aarde hebben gevormd.

1. CENTRAL

2. EAST

3. WEST

4. NORTH

5. SOUTH

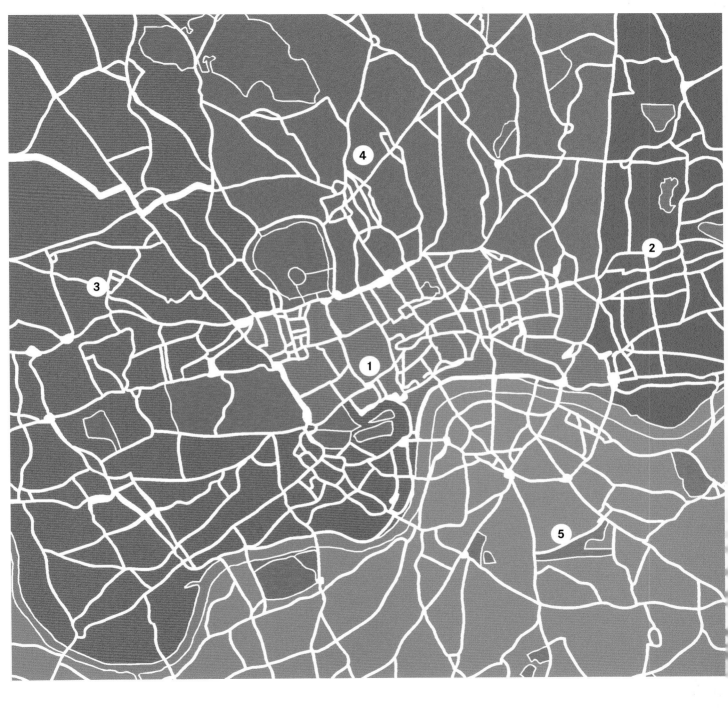

(1) CENTRAL

(2) EAST

(4) NORTH

(5) SOUTH

CENTRAL

Dress by
Dress

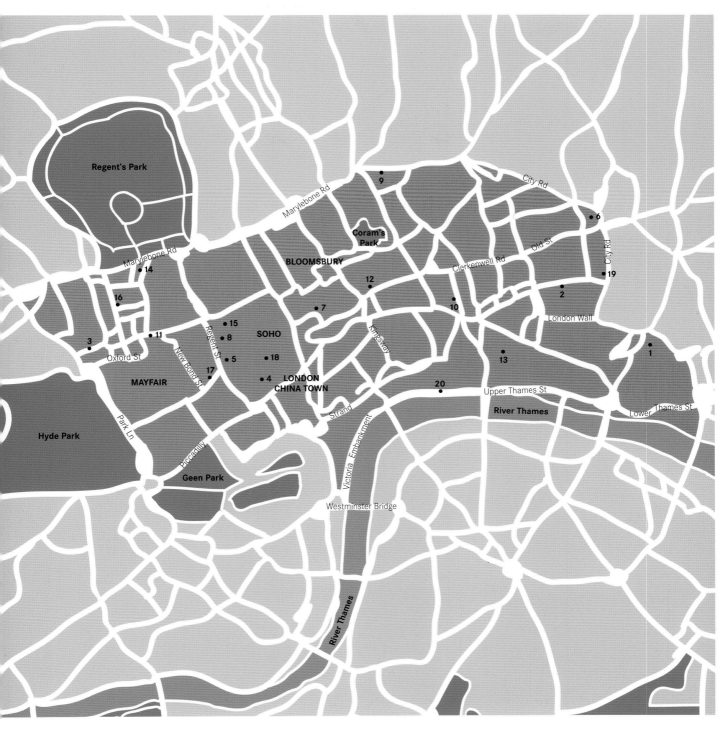

WORK

30 St Mary Axe ①

Southwark

Foster and Partners
www.fosterandpartners.com

Photos: © Foster + Partners

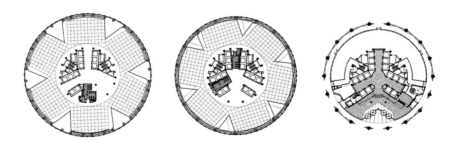

Floor plans

Popularly known as the Gherkin, the cone-shaped 590-foot-tall structure reduces wind turbulence around the building. The design allows it to produce important energy savings on lighting and ventilation.

Der Londoner Volksmund hat diesen Büroturm „The Gherkin" getauft, die Gurke. Die Spindelform hilft, die Luftturbulenzen um das Gebäude herum zu verringern. Beim Bau des Wolkenkratzers wurde auch Wert darauf gelegt, bei Beleuchtung und Lüftung Energie zu sparen.

Populairement baptisée le Gherkin (« le cornichon »), cette tour de 180 mètres de haut a une forme conique qui réduit les turbulences du vent. Ce design permet de grandes économies d'énergie en matière d'éclairage et de ventilation.

In de volksmond heet hij The Gherkin (de augurk), deze 180 meter hoge toren. Door zijn conische vorm heeft het gebouw minder last van de wind. Het ontwerp is zodanig dat er veel energie bespaard wordt op verlichting en ventilatie.

SEE

Barbican Arts Centre ②

Silk Street

Allford Hall Monaghan Morris
www.ahmm.co.uk

Photos: © Rob Parrish

The common areas and transit zones around this famous art center were remodeled and expanded to facilitate public access. As well as the new entrances, the designer furniture and lighting shore up the original character of the building.

Die Erschließungs- und Gemeinschaftsräume dieses berühmten Kunstzentrums wurden umgebaut und erweitert, um dem Publikum den Zugang zu erleichtern. Neben den neuen Eingängen verleihen auch das Mobiliar und die Beleuchtung dem Gebäude seine eigene Prägung.

En vue de simplifier l'accès du public, les espaces communs et de circulation de ce célèbre centre d'art ont été rénovés et élargis. Outre les nouveaux accès, le mobilier et l'éclairage design accentuent l'originalité du bâtiment.

Om het gebouw voor het publiek toegankelijker te maken, werden de doorgangs- en gemeenschappelijke ruimten van dit beroemde kunstcentrum gerenoveerd en uitgebreid. Niet alleen de nieuwe toegangsruimten, ook het meubilair en de designverlichting versterken het karakter van het gebouw.

LEARN

Hampden Gurney ③

Nutford Place

BDP
www.bdp.com

Photos: © Martine Hamilton

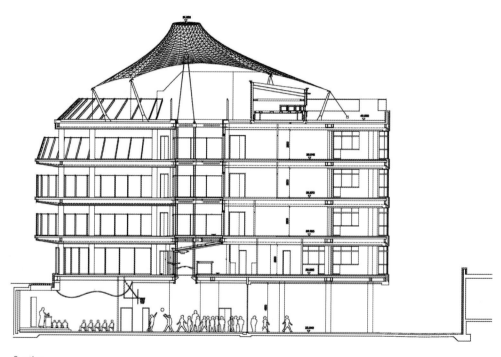

Section

On the site where a 1950 school building stood, the architects have raised two new six-story constructions: one to house the Hampden Gurney School and the other in the shape of an 'L', with 52 apartments in what used to be the playground. The new courtyard, now covered, is housed in each of the floors of the new school building.

Anstelle eines Schulgebäudes aus den fünfziger Jahren haben die Architekten zwei sechsgeschossige Neubauten errichtet: Einer nimmt die Hampden Gurney Schule auf und der andere, in L-Form über dem ehemaligen Spiel- und Pausenhof errichtet, beherbergt 52 Wohnungen. Für die Pausen steht nun in jeder Etage des Schulneubaus ein überdachter Raum zur Verfügung.

Là où se dressait une école de 1950, les architectes ont construit deux nouveaux bâtiments de six étages : l'un pour accueillir l'école Hampden Gurney, l'autre en forme de « L » avec 52 appartements, à la place de l'ancienne cour de récréation. La nouvelle cour, maintenant couverte, est présente à chaque étage du nouveau bâtiment scolaire.

Op de plek waar een schoolgebouw uit de jaren vijftig stond, hebben de architecten twee nieuwe gebouwen van zes verdiepingen neergezet. In het ene gebouw is de Hampden Gurney school gehuisvest. In het andere, L-vormige gebouw bevinden zich 52 appartementen. De nieuwe, nu overdekte binnenplaats is doorgetrokken naar alle verdiepingen van het nieuwe schoolgebouw.

EAT

Snog Soho ④

9 Brewer Street

Cinimod Studio
www.cinimodstudio.com

Photos: © Cinimod Studio

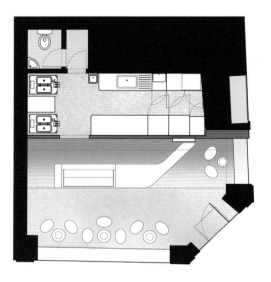

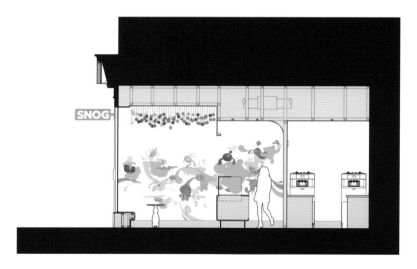

Floor plan and section

The interior design of this store which sells nothing but frozen yoghurt recalls an endless summer. The floor boasts a photograph of grass and the ceiling comprises 700 glass bubbles with led lighting that change color to generate different ambiences.

Die Innengestaltung dieses Ladenlokals, in dem nur Joghurteiscreme verkauft wird, lässt an einen endlosen Sommer denken. Den Boden bildet eine Rasenfotografie und die Decke besteht aus 700 Glasblasen mit LED-Leuchten, die ständig die Farbe wechseln und neue Eindrücke schaffen.

Le design d'intérieur de ce magasin, vendant uniquement des yaourts glacés évoque un été sans fin. Le sol est recouvert de la photographie d'un gazon, et le plafond compte 700 bulles en verre avec des LED qui changent de couleur pour créer diverses atmosphères.

Het interieur van deze winkel die uitsluitend yoghurtijs verkoopt, roept de sfeer van een eeuwige zomer op. De vloer is een foto van een grasveld en het plafond bestaat uit 700 glazen bellen met ledlampen die steeds een andere sfeer scheppen doordat ze van kleur veranderen.

SHOP

Fornarina Store (5)

30 Carnaby St

Giorgio Borruso Design
www.borrusodesign.com

Photos: © Benny Chan/Fotoworks

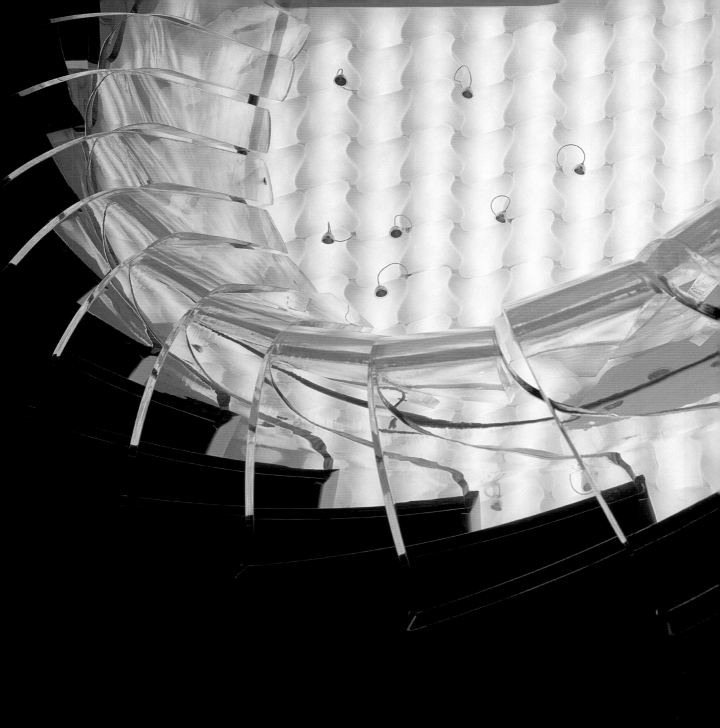

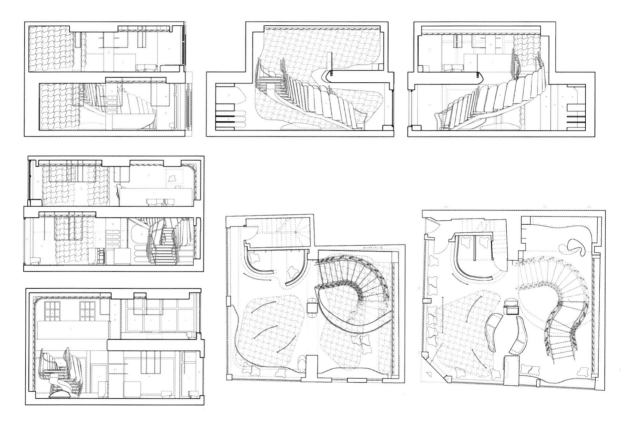

Sections   Floor plans

This 1,700-sq-ft store resembles a strange organism with walls and ceilings covered in a shiny membrane comprising over 1,000 asymmetrical backlit pieces. Some of them emerge from the wall to form seats or pedestals.

Dieses Geschäft umfasst 160 Quadratmeter und wirkt wie ein seltsamer Organismus. Wände und Decke sind mit einer leuchtenden Membran bedeckt, die aus über 1000 asymmetrischen, von der Rückseite her beleuchteten Teilen besteht. Zuweilen löst sich eines dieser Teile aus der Wand und wird zu einem Sitz oder Podest.

Ce magasin de 160 m^2 ressemble à un étrange organisme avec ses murs et ses plafonds recouverts d'une membrane lumineuse faite de 1 000 pièces asymétriques rétroéclairées. Certaines pièces sortent du mur pour former des sièges ou des piédestaux.

Deze winkel van 160 vierkante meter lijkt met zijn wanden en plafonds, die bekleed zijn met een lichtgevend membraan bestaande uit ruim 1000 door backlight verlichte asymmetrische vormen, op een vreemd organisme. Enkele vormen kunnen uit de muur gehaald worden en dienen als zitplaatsen of voetstukken.

HEAL

The Richard Desmond (6) Children's Eye Centre

162 City Road

Penoyre & Prasad
www.penoyre-prasad.net

Photos: © Lyndon Douglas; Moorley Von Sternberg; Theodore Wood

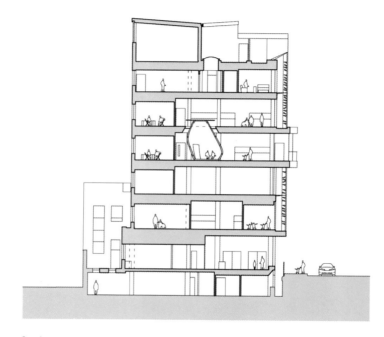

Section

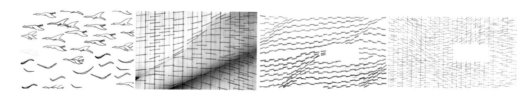

Sketch

The design of this children's ophthalmology center took the features of its clients into account. Large open spaces, attractively colored corners and extensive games areas help turn a possibly traumatic experience into something positive.

Bei der Planung dieses Zentrums für Augenheilkunde für Kinder standen die Bedürfnisse der kleinen Nutzer im Vordergrund. Deshalb wurden offene, weitläufige Räume mit attraktiver Farbgestaltung geschaffen und große Spielzonen eingerichtet, um aus einer oft traumatischen Erfahrung eine positive zu machen.

Dans le design de ce centre ophtalmologique pour enfants, les caractéristiques des usagers ont été prises en compte. Des espaces généreux et ouverts, des recoins aux couleurs attirantes et de grandes zones de jeux permettent de rendre agréable une expérience éventuellement traumatisante.

Bij het ontwerp van dit oogheelkundige centrum voor kinderen is rekening gehouden met de gebruikertjes van het gebouw. Er zijn ruime, open ruimten, vrolijke kleuren en grote speelruimten die helpen een mogelijk traumatische ervaring te veranderen in een positieve gebeurtenis.

SEE

The Great Court at the British Museum ⑦

Great Russell St

Foster and Partners
www.fosterandpartners.com

Photos: © Foster + Partners

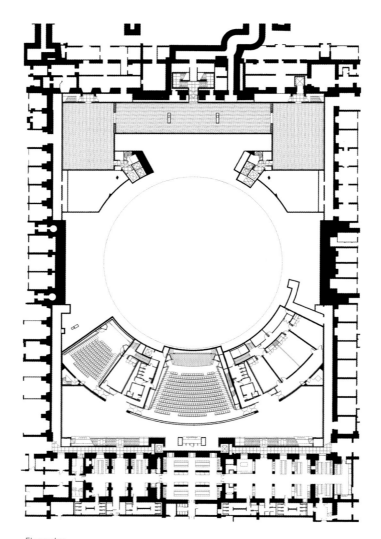

Floor plan

The remodeling of the central courtyard of the British Museum was designed with the goal of organizing the transit of visitors and recovering a space that lacked identity. The works included the installation of a steel and glass roof that unites the various buildings and the restoration of the façade and Reading Room.

Bei der Neugestaltung des Innenhofs des Britischen Museums standen die Regulierung der Besucherströme und die Rückgewinnung eines bis dahin ungenutzten Raums im Mittelpunkt. Die einzelnen Teile des Gebäudes wurden durch das Dach aus Stahl und Glas miteinander verbunden sowie die Fassaden und der runde Lesesaal restauriert.

La rénovation de la cour centrale du British Museum avait pour objectif d'organiser le déplacement des visiteurs et de récupérer un espace dénué d'identité. Les travaux ont inclus l'installation d'un toit en acier et verre reliant les différents bâtiments, ainsi que la restauration de la façade et de la salle de lecture.

De nieuwe centrale binnenplaats van het British Museum moest zorgen voor een goede doorstroom van bezoekers en moest de ruimte weer een eigen karakter geven. Hij kreeg een overhuiving van glas en staal die de verschillende gebouwen met elkaar verbindt. Verder werden de gevel en de leeszaal gerestaureerd.

WORK

West End House 8

11 Hills Place

3DReid
www.3dreid.com

Photos: © Andrew Southall/3DReid

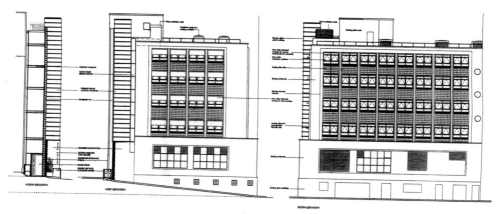

Elevation

A 1950s office building was renovated to house the offices of the architects 3DReid. The glass façade that runs the length of the five floors and the elevator tower, which is lit at night, catch the eye of passersby in busy downtown Oxford Street.

Ein Bürogebäude aus den fünfziger Jahren wurde umgebaut, um die Arbeitsräume des Architekturbüros 3DReid aufzunehmen. Die über fünf Geschosse verglaste Fassade und der nachts beleuchtete Fahrstuhlschacht ziehen die Blicke der Passanten auf der belebten Oxford Street an.

Un immeuble de bureaux des années 50 a été rénové pour accueillir les bureaux des architectes 3DReid. La façade vitrée sur cinq étages et la tour de l'ascenseur éclairée la nuit attirent l'attention des passants à proximité sur Oxford Street.

Om het architectenbureau 3DReid te huisvesten werd een kantoorgebouw uit de jaren vijftig gerenoveerd. De blik van voorbijgangers in de op slechts enkele meters afstand gelegen Oxford Street wordt getrokken naar de glazen gevel – over alle vijf verdiepingen – en naar de liftschacht, die 's avonds verlicht is.

LIVE

Field Street 9

1–6 Field Street

Project Orange
www.projectorange.com

Photos: © Gareth Gardner

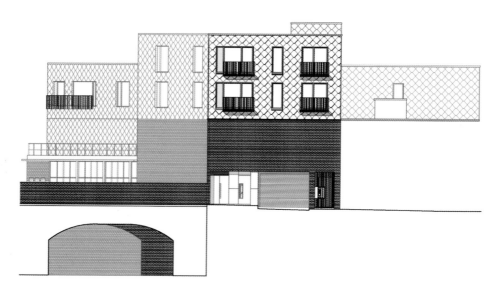

Elevation

This three-story building houses a music rehearsal room and a home and is the result of the expansion of the property. The new building sits on the old roof and is differentiated by a façade clad in rusted copper.

Dieser dreigeschossige Bau beherbergt eine Wohnung und Proberäume und ist als Erweiterung eines bestehenden Gebäudes entstanden. Der Neubau wurde auf dem Dach des Altbaus errichtet, von dem er sich durch die mit oxydierten Kupferplatten verkleidete Fassade abhebt.

Ce bâtiment de trois étages, qui renferme une salle de répétitions et un logement, est le fruit de l'agrandissement d'une propriété. La nouvelle construction repose sur l'ancien toit et se distingue par sa façade revêtue de cuivre oxydé.

Dit gebouw van drie verdiepingen, een uitbreiding van een bestaand pand, huisvest een muziekoefenruimte en een woning. De nieuwe constructie rust op het dak van de oude constructie, en wordt ervan onderscheiden door zijn gevel van geoxideerd koper.

SHOP

Holts Lapidary 10

98 Hatton Garden

Blauel Architects
www.blauel.com

Photos: © Dennis Gilbert/View

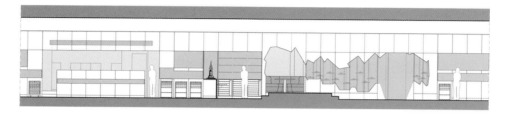

Internal elevation

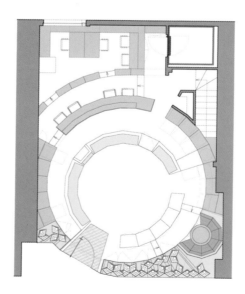

Layout

This store window resembles a fissure in a rock that enables a glimpse of the precious stones inside. The concentric design places the customer in the middle of a rainbow of gems distributed in the display cases.

Das Schaufenster dieses Geschäfts erscheint wie eine Felsspalte, in der die ausgestellten Edelsteine sichtbar werden. Das konzentrisch angelegte Design stellt den Betrachter in die Achse eines Regenbogens, der von den Juwelen der Vitrinen gebildet wird.

La vitrine de ce magasin ressemble à une faille dans la roche révélant les pierres précieuses qu'elle renferme. Le design concentrique plonge le client dans un arc-en-ciel de gemmes réparties sur les présentoirs.

De etalage van deze winkel lijkt op een spleet in een rots, waardoor de kostbare stenen binnen te zien zijn. Door het concentrische ontwerp wordt de klant in het midden van een regenboog van de in de vitrines liggende edelstenen geplaatst.

SHOP

Reiss HQ ⑪

9-12 Barrett Street

Squire and Partners
www.squireandpartners.com

Photos: © William Pryce

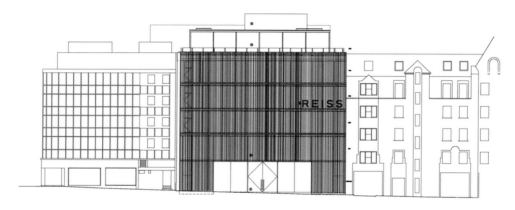

Elevation

The skin of this building, the global headquarters of fashion chain Reiss, comprises layers of glass and acrylic that regulate the inside temperature. The vertical sheets of the outer layer shimmer with led lighting and generate a luminous façade visible from yards around.

Die Außenhaut dieses Gebäudes der Modefirma Reiss besteht aus übereinander liegenden Schichten aus Glas und Acryl, die helfen die Innentemperatur zu regeln. Die senkrechten Lamellen vor der Fassade werden über LED-Leuchten erhellt und strahlen mehrere Meter weit hinaus.

La peau de ce bâtiment, siège de la marque de mode Reiss, est faite de couches en verre et en acrylique régulant la température intérieure. Les lames verticales de la couche externe sont éclairées avec des LED, ce qui donne une façade lumineuse visible à la ronde.

De huid van dit gebouw, hoofdkantoor van modehuis Reiss, bestaat uit lagen van glas en acryl die de temperatuur binnen regelen. De verticale platen van de buitenste laag hebben ledverlichting waardoor een verlichte gevel ontstaat die rondom op vele meters afstand zichtbaar is.

WORK

MediaCom Headquarters ⑫

124 Theobalds Road

ORMS
www.orms.co.uk

Photos: © James Brittain

In contrast with the outside of the building, the inside of the former headquarters of the Cable & Wireless company which today houses an advertising agency has been totally overhauled with bright colors and stimulating spaces. The amenities are distributed over four floors that can be seen from a striking central atrium with a statuesque staircase.

Während das Äußere des ehemaligen Gebäudes von Cable & Wireless unverändert erhalten blieb, wurde das Innere mit lebhaften Farben und anregenden Raumschöpfungen völlig umgestaltet. Heute ist in dem viergeschossigen Bau eine Werbefirma untergebracht, deren Räumlichkeiten vom eindrucksvollen zentralen Innenhof mit seiner mächtigen Treppe aus einzusehen sind.

Tranchant avec l'extérieur du bâtiment, l'intérieur de l'ancien siège social de l'entreprise Cable & Wireless, hébergeant aujourd'hui une agence de publicité, a été entièrement rénové avec des couleurs intenses et des espaces stimulants. Les installations sont distribuées sur quatre étages visibles depuis une impressionnante cour centrale, avec son escalier sculptural.

Het interieur van het voormalige hoofdkantoor van Cable & Wireless, waarin nu een reclamebureau is gehuisvest, is volledig gerenoveerd. De fel gekleurde ruimten vormen een levendig contrast met de buitenkant van het gebouw. De voorzieningen zijn verdeeld over vier verdiepingen, die vanuit het imposante centrale atrium zichtbaar zijn.

WORK

Old Bailey 13

7-10 Old Bailey

Avery Associates Architects
www.avery-architects.co.uk

Photos: © Avery Associates Architects

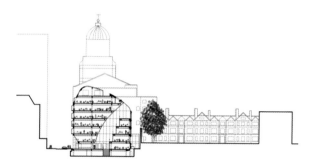

Section

Sited in a zone of protected buildings, this office block maintains the proportions of the neighboring volumes. The round atrium lets natural light directly into the entrance lobby.

Dieses Bürogebäude wurde in einem geschützten Baubereich errichtet und musste sich daher an den Proportionen der umlegenden Gebäude ausrichten. Durch das runde Atrium fällt das Tageslicht in die Eingangshalle.

Situé dans une zone de constructions protégées, ce bâtiment de bureaux conserve les proportions des volumes voisins. La cour arrondie favorise l'entrée directe de lumière naturelle dans le hall d'entrée.

Dit kantoorgebouw staat in een gebied met beschermde gebouwen en heeft de verhoudingen van de belendende bouwwerken gehandhaafd. Het atrium met zijn ronde vormen laat het daglicht rechtstreeks de entreehal binnenkomen.

LEARN

St Marylebone School (14)

64 Marylebone High Street

Gumuchdjian Architects
www.gumuchdjian.com

Photos: © Morely von Sternberg; Richard Davies

This school needed to expand its gym, dance studios and music and art departments. The shortage of land at the sides was resolved with new underground buildings beneath the two public courtyards.

Um den Platzmangel dieser Schule auf ihrem engen Grundstück zu beheben, wurden unter den beiden öffentlich zugänglichen Pausenhöfen neue Räume für Gymnastik- und Tanzstunden, Musik- und Kunstunterricht geschaffen.

Cette école avait besoin d'installations plus grandes pour des gymnases, des salles de danse et des classes de musique et d'art. Pour pallier le manque de terrain sur les côtés, de nouvelles constructions souterraines ont vu le jour en dessous des deux cours ouvertes au public.

De faciliteiten van deze school moesten worden uitgebreid met gymzalen, dansstudio's, en muziek- en kunstafdelingen. Het ruimteprobleem in de breedterichting werd opgelost door naar beneden uit te bouwen, onder de openbare ruimte van twee binnenplaatsen.

WORK

Hills Place ⑮

10 Hills Place

AL_A team
www.amandalevetearchitects.com

Photos: © Gidon Fuehrer

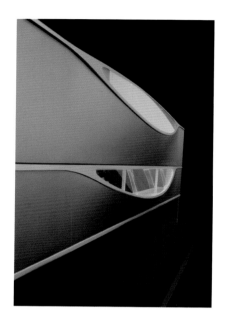

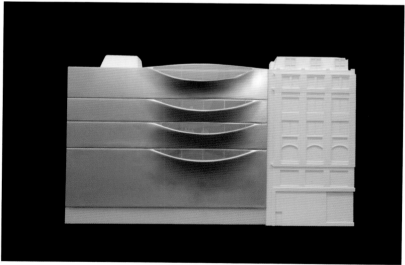

Models

To create the sculptural façade of this office building, the designers used technology normally employed in ship-building. The aluminum and glass skin faces upward to maximize the entry of natural light.

Für die Gestaltung dieser ausdrucksstarken Fassade griff man auf die Verfahren der Bootsbautechnik zurück. Die Außenhaut aus Glas und Aluminium öffnet sich nach oben hin und erlaubt so den größtmöglichen Lichteinfall.

Pour dresser la façade sculpturale de cet immeuble de bureaux, la même technologie que celle intervenant dans la construction de bateaux a été employée. La peau en aluminium et en verre est orientée vers le ciel pour optimiser l'entrée de lumière naturelle.

Voor de sculpturale gevel van dit kantoorgebouw werd technologie uit de scheepsbouw gebruikt. De huid van aluminium en glas is gericht op de hemel, om zoveel mogelijk daglicht te laten binnenkomen.

EAT

Canteen Baker Street 16

55 Baker Street, W1U 8EW

Canteen's in-house design team

Photos: © courtesy of Canteen

The inspiration for the restaurant design draws on public and common spaces such as schools, libraries and municipal buildings that speak to the optimism of the mid-20th century. Simple and noble long-lasting materials were used in the construction.

Für die Ausstattung dieses Restaurants ließen sich die Innenarchitekten von den optimistischen Gestaltungsmustern für öffentliche Gebäude wie Schulen, Bibliotheken oder Rathäuser inspirieren, wie sie um die Mitte des 20. Jhs. üblich waren. Verwendet wurden einfache und edle haltbare Materialien.

L'inspiration pour le design de ce restaurant provient des espaces publics, tels qu'écoles, bibliothèques et bâtiments municipaux, à l'image de l'optimisme du milieu du XXe siècle. Sont pour cela intervenus des matériaux simples et nobles de longue durée.

Het ontwerp van dit restaurant is geïnspireerd op openbare gebouwen zoals scholen, bibliotheken en gemeentehuizen die verwijzen naar het optimisme van de jaren vijftig van de 20e eeuw. Er werden daarom eenvoudige, duurzame materialen gebruikt.

EAT

Sketch 17

9 Conduit Street, W1S 2XG

Noe Duchaufour Lawrence
www.neonata.fr

Photos: © courtesy of Neonata

Sketch, one of London's most upscale restaurants, is located in a remodeled 18th-century building. The two floors house different spaces that unite food, art and music. The interior design appeals to the senses, with original shapes and colors that complete an almost surreal ambiance.

Das Sketch gehört zu den teuersten Restaurants Londons. Es befindet sich in einem umgebauten Haus aus dem 18. Jh. Auf zwei Etagen kann man Essen, Kunst und Musik genießen. Die Inneneinrichtung mit ihren originellen Formen und Farben schafft ein nahezu surrealistisches Ambiente und spricht alle Sinne an.

Sketch, l'un des restaurants les plus chers de Londres, se trouve dans un bâtiment restauré du XVIIIe siècle. Ses deux étages renferment différents espaces mariant gastronomie, art et musique. Le design intérieur éveille les sens, avec des formes et des couleurs originales venant compléter une atmosphère quasi surréaliste.

Het chique restaurant Sketch bevindt zich in een gerenoveerd 18e-eeuws gebouw. Op de twee verdiepingen zijn ruimten ondergebracht waar je van een maaltijd, muziek of kunst kunt genieten. Het interieurontwerp prikkelt de zintuigen met zijn originele vormen en kleuren die de bijna surrealistische sfeer aanvullen.

EAT

Inamo (18)

134–136 Wardour Street, W1F 8ZP

Blacksheep
www.blacksheepweb.com

Photos: © courtesy of Inamo

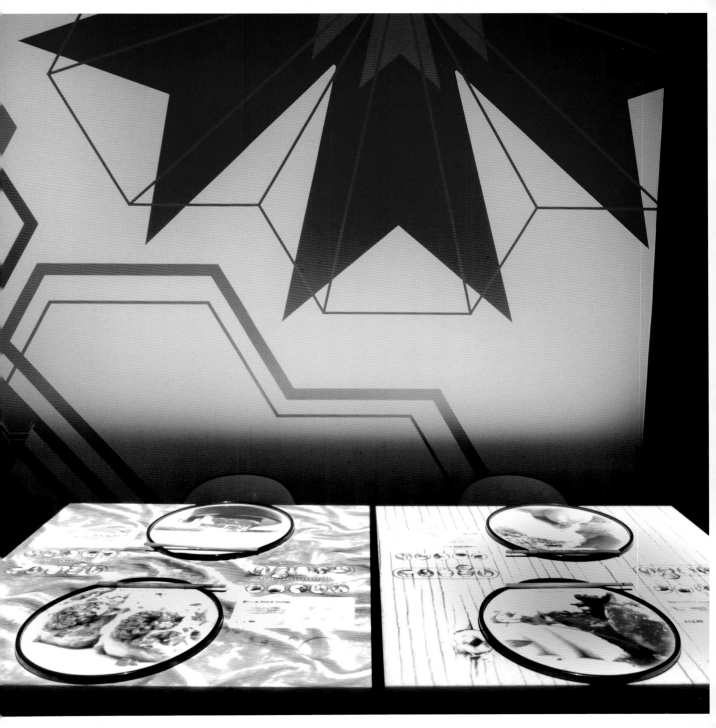

This pan-Asian restaurant and bar features interactive menus projected onto individual screens above each table. As well as surfing the food and drink options, diners can see the chefs at work and find information on the neighborhood.

In diesem Restaurant wird Essen aus ganz Asien angeboten. Die Speisenfolge ist interaktiv zu gestalten und wird von entsprechenden Apparaten auf jeden Tisch projiziert. Die Gäste können nicht nur durch das Angebot von Speisen und Getränken surfen, sondern auch den Köchen bei der Arbeit zusehen und sich über das Viertel informieren.

Dans ce restaurant et bar de cuisine panasiatique, les menus sont interactifs et projetés sur des écrans individuels au-dessus de chaque table. À part naviguer parmi les choix de plats et de boissons, les convives peuvent observer les chefs travailler en temps réel et s'informer sur le quartier.

In deze Aziatische bar annex restaurant zijn de menu's interactief. Elke tafel heeft een eigen terminal. Daarmee kunnen niet alleen de verschillende gerechten en drankjes worden uitgezocht, maar zijn bovendien de koks in real time aan het werk te zien, en kun je informatie over de buurt vinden.

WORK

201 Bishopsgate and (19) The Broadgate Tower

Worship Street and Bishopsgate

Skidmore, Owings & Merrill (SOM)
www.som.com

Photos: © Skidmore, Owings & Merrill; Richard Leeney / British Land

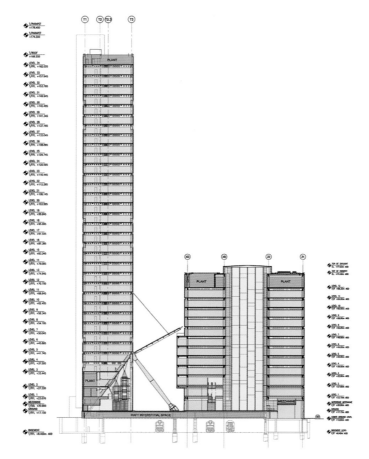

Elevation

Located in the heart of the City, the two buildings, one of 12 stories and the other of 35, are connected by a glassed-in public gallery. The shapes were influenced by the plaque marking the foundation above the old tracks of Liverpool Station and the views to St Paul's Cathedral, which limited the height of the building.

Die beiden Gebäude befinden sich im Herzen der Londoner City. Sie sind 12 bzw. 35 Stockwerke hoch und über eine öffentlich zugängliche Galerie miteinander verbunden. Beim Entwurf musste auf die Tunneldecke über den ehemaligen Gleisen des Liverpooler Bahnhofs und, was die Bauhöhe angeht, auf die Sichtbeziehungen zur nahen St Pauls Cathedral Rücksicht genommen werden.

Situés en plein cœur de la City, les deux bâtiments (de 12 et 35 étages) sont reliés par une galerie publique vitrée. Les formes ont subi l'influence de la plaque de fondations dessus des anciennes voies de la gare de Liverpool, ainsi que des vues de la cathédrale St Paul qui ont limité la hauteur de la construction.

Deze twee gebouwen midden in de City, een van 12 en een van 35 verdiepingen, zijn met elkaar verbonden door een glazen galerij. De vorm werd mede bepaald door de funderingsplaat boven de oude spoorbaan van Liverpool Station, en door het uitzicht op St Paul's Cathedral, waardoor de hoogte beperkt bleef.

LINK

Millennium Bridge (20)

Southwark, EC4V

Foster and Partners
www.fosterandpartners.com

Photos: © Foster + Partners

Elevation

This 1,000-foot-long bridge joins the Tate Modern Gallery with the City. It has two support platforms and is made in three sections. The eight cables with diameters of 4.7 inches that keep the bridge suspended can support a weight of up to 2,000 tons.

Die 325 Meter lange Fußgängerbrücke verbindet die Londoner City mit der Tate Modern Gallery auf dem anderen Themseufer. Die Struktur ruht auf zwei Stützplattformen und ist in drei Abschnitte unterteilt. Acht 12 cm starke Stahlseile halten die Brücke in der Schwebe. Sie sind darauf ausgelegt, ein Gewicht von 2000 Tonnen zu tragen.

Ce pont de 325 mètres de long relie la Tate Modern Gallery à la City. Doté de deux plates-formes de soutien, il compte trois sections. Les huit câbles de 12 cm de diamètre qui maintiennent le pont en suspension sont tendus pour supporter jusqu'à 2 000 tonnes de poids.

Deze brug van 325 meter lengte verbindt het Tate Modern met de Londense City. Hij heeft twee ondersteunende platforms en bestaat uit drie delen. De acht kabels van 12 cm dikte waaraan de brug is opgehangen, kunnen tot 2000 ton gewicht dragen.

EAST

Hackney
Downs

Wanstead
Park

↑ 16

London
Fields

Victoria
Park

Kingsland Rd

● 4

● 1

● 12

Hackney Rd

5

Shoreditch High St

● 9

Columbia Rd

6

Old St

● 10

Bethnal Green Rd

7

City Rd

14

● 15

Bishopsgate

Commercial St

Brick Lane

White Chapel Rd

● 11

● 8

Commercial Rd

W India Dock Rd   Aspen Way

13

River Thames

River Thames

● 2

● 3

Mudchute
Park

Milwall
Park

Isle of Dogs

SHOP

Old Spitalfields Market ①

Brushfield and Commercial Streets

Jestico + Whiles
www.jesticowhiles.com

Photos: © Gwynne Jones

SPITALFIELDS, DEAR READER? NO DOUBT YOU HAVE – AN IMPRESSION THAT... STREETS, LYING LIKE NARROW BLACK... STEEPLES, SOMEWHERE ABOUT... WHERESALLOW, UNSHORN... HAVE NOTHING TO DO, PROWL LANGUIDLY ABOUT,... OR SIT BROODING ON DOOR STEPS, AND... ASSEMBLE TOGETHER IN A CROWD TO PETITION... THE QUEEN, AFTER WHICH THERE IS A DRAWING-... COURT BALL, WHERE ALL THE GREAT LADIES WEAR... SPITALFIELDS MANUFACTURE AND THEN THE WEAVERS... A DAY OR TWO, AND SO RELAPSE INTO PROWLING ABOUT... LEANING AGAINST THE POSTS, AND BROODING ON... DOORSTEPS. CHARLES DICKENS, 1851

...HAND GRENADES... WOODEN BOXES LIKE AMMUNITION... BUT THE ARTILLERY GROUND IS... OF LORRIES UNLOADING MORE FRUIT... SMELLED OF CAMEL, BANANAS IN VAST... SWINGING FROM THEIR HOOKS, THE... LEATHER AND SILVER, JUNK AND ANTIQUES... BECAUSE SPITALFIELDS WAS A WEAVERS PLACE... PLACE, A BORDER CROSSING OF GOODS AND... EVERYTHING THAT SPITALFIELDS HAS BEEN IT IS... TIME, BUT PROTEAN IN ITS ENERGY. GHOSTS... STREET DOORWAY, YET THE OFFICES, DELIS, RESTA... AND MARKET STALLS ARE ARMIES OF NEW LIFE THIS... OWN ALCHEMY. JEANETTE WINTERSON 2007

The renovation of Spitalfields Market, one of the best-preserved examples of Victorian architecture, included improving the commercial areas and creating a flexible space for cultural activities.

Die Restaurierung der Markthalle von Spitalfields, einer der besterhaltenen aus viktorianischer Zeit, sah auch die Verbesserung der Verkaufsflächen und die Schaffung eines Mehrzweckraums für kulturelle Veranstaltungen vor.

La rénovation du marché de Spitalfields, l'un des mieux conservés de style victorien, a amélioré les espaces commerciaux et créé une zone modulable pour des activités culturelles.

De restauratie van Spitalfields Market, een van de best bewaarde markten in victoriaanse stijl, omvatte onder meer het opknappen van het marktterrein en de aanleg van een flexibel gebied voor culturele activiteiten.

TRAVEL

New DLR Station for Heron Quays ②

Canary Wharf

Alsop Architects
www.alsoparchitects.com

Photos: © Morely von Sternberg

This train station, 88 feet wide, 275 feet long and 52 feet high, is located at Canary Wharf and connects with the Jubilee Place shopping mall. The space, with stainless steel walls and roofs, houses a cement shell that sustains the viaduct along which the trains run.

Der Bahnhof liegt in Canary Wharf und ist mit dem Einkaufszentrum Jubilee Place verbunden. Die Anlage ist 84 Meter lang, 27 Meter breit und 16 Meter hoch. Unter der Edelstahlverkleidung der Wände und der Decke verbirgt sich eine Betonstruktur, die den Viadukt stützt, auf dem die Züge verkehren.

Cette gare de 27 mètres de large, 84 de long et 16 de haut se trouve à Canary Wharf et est connectée au centre commercial Jubilee Place. L'espace, dont les murs et les plafonds sont en acier inoxydable, possède une carapace en ciment soutenant le viaduc par lequel passe le train.

Vanuit het station van 27 meter breed, 84 meter lang en 16 meter hoog in Canary Wharf is de shopping mall van Jubilee Place te bereiken. Het betonnen schild van de ruimte, die wanden en daken van roestvrij staal heeft, draagt het viaduct waar de treinen doorheen rijden.

SHOP

Jubilee Place ③

Canary Wharf

BDP
www.bdp.com

Model

The glass roof of this shopping mall not only provides natural light but also boasts stunning views of the ever-changing landscape of Canary Wharf. From here you can also access the Underground station and the passageways that connect with the buildings.

Das Glasdach des Einkaufszentrums lässt nicht nur das Tageslicht einfallen, sondern erlaubt auch einzigartige Ausblicke auf die sich ständig verändernde Stadtlandschaft der Canary Wharf. Über Verbindungsgänge sind die U-Bahn und die angrenzenden Gebäude zu erreichen.

Le toit vitré de ce centre commercial laisse entrer la lumière naturelle et offre des vues privilégiées du paysage changeant de Canary Wharf. Il s'agit aussi d'un point d'accès à la station de métro et aux couloirs communiquant avec les bâtiments.

Het glazen dak van dit winkelcentrum zorgt niet alleen voor daglicht, maar biedt ook een prachtig uitzicht op het altijd wisselende stadslandschap van Canary Wharf. Van hieruit zijn ook het metrostation en diverse paden die de gebouwen met elkaar verbinden bereikbaar.

LIVE

Adelaide Wharf (4)

Regent's Canal

Allford Hall Monaghan Morris
www.ahmm.co.uk

Photos: © Timothy Soar

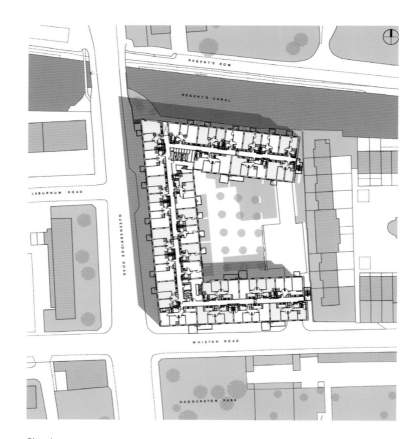

Site plan

This block of 147 apartments and offices creates a U-shaped courtyard in front of the canal. Each apartment has an outdoor area that projects over the street. The façade is covered in sheets of wood as a nod to the packaging warehouses that formerly stood there.

Dieser Block umfasst 147 Appartements und Büros und öffnet sich zum Kanal hin zu einem U-förmigen Hof. Zu jedem Appartement gehört ein Außenraum, der vor der Fassade über der Straße schwebt. Die Fassade mit ihrer Holzverkleidung erinnert an die Lagerhäuser mit ihren Verpackungskisten, die sich früher hier befanden.

Ce bloc de 147 appartements et bureaux ouvre une cour en « U » face au canal. Chaque appartement compte un espace extérieur surplombant la rue. La façade du bâtiment est revêtue de planche en bois à l'image des entrepôts d'emballages anciennement dans cette zone.

Door de vorm van dit gebouwenblok met 147 appartementen en kantoren is een U-vormige binnenplaats tegenover het water ontstaan. Elk appartement heeft een buitenruimte die boven de straat hangt. De gevel is bekleed met houten platen, een herinnering aan de pakhuizen met verpakkingsmaterialen die hier ooit stonden.

LIVE

Wakering Road Foyer ⑤

50 Wakering Road

Jestico + Whiles
www.jesticowhiles.com

Photos: © Nikhilesh Haval

This building has 116 beds for marginalized young people. The volume lets sunlight in while protecting the living quarters and offices from street noise. The 'L' shape comprises two blocks and boasts one garden at ground level and another on the roof.

In diesem Gebäude stehen 116 Betten für ausgegrenzte Jugendliche zur Verfügung. Obwohl der Einfall des Sonnenlichts gefördert wird, sind die Wohneinheiten und Büros zur Straße hin gegen den Lärm isoliert. Der Komplex in L-Form umfasst eine Grünanlage zu ebener Erde und einen Dachgarten.

Ce bâtiment offre 116 lits aux jeunes en situation d'exclusion. Le volume permet l'entrée de lumière naturelle tout en isolant les logements et les bureaux du bruit de la rue. Sa forme en « L » faite de deux blocs dégage un jardin au niveau du sol et un autre sur le toit.

Dit opvanghuis telt 116 bedden voor jongeren. Er valt veel daglicht binnen, terwijl de vertrekken en kantoren tegelijkertijd geïsoleerd zijn tegen het straatlawaai. Door de L-vorm die de twee blokken maken, is zowel op de begane grond als op het dak een tuin ontstaan.

LIVE

Tanner Street ⑥

Barking

Jestico + Whiles
www.jesticowhiles.com

Photos: © Morley Von Sternberg

Model

This block of 165 low-cost apartments has an unusual façade for the area and connects an isolated residential zone with the public facilities and leisure options of Barking Town.

In diesem Gebäudekomplex mit seiner für die Umgebung ungewöhnlichen Fassade befinden sich 165 preiswerte Wohnungen. Die Anlage schafft einen Übergang zwischen einer abgelegenen Wohngegend und den kommunalen und Freizeiteinrichtungen des Zentrums von Barking Town.

Ce bloc de 165 logements à loyers modérés présente une façade inhabituelle pour l'endroit. Il connecte une zone résidentielle isolée aux installations publiques et de loisirs de Barking Town.

In dit gebouwencomplex, met een voor de wijk opvallende gevel, zijn 165 goedkope woningen ondergebracht. Het complex verbindt een geïsoleerd woongebied met overheids- en amusementsvoorzieningen van het centrum van Barking Town.

LIVE

Axe Street (7)

Barking

Jestico + Whiles
www.jesticowhiles.com

Photos: © Tim Crocker

Ground floor plan

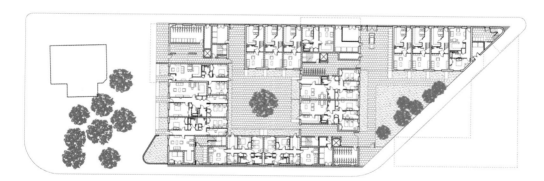

First floor plan

As part of the regeneration plan for Barking and Dagenham, this building which houses 93 apartments is sited on land formerly occupied by a car park. The staggered façade is clad in bricks on one side and copper on the other.

Im Rahmen des Stadterneuerungsprogramms für Barking und Dagenham wurde anstelle eines Parkplatzes dieses Gebäude mit 93 Wohnungen errichtet. Die abgestufte Fassade ist auf der einen Seite mit Backstein und auf der anderen mit Kupfer verkleidet.

Dans le cadre d'un plan de transformation de Barking y Dagenham, ce bâtiment de 93 logements se dresse sur le terrain auparavant occupé par un parking. La façade de la structure en escaliers est recouverte de briques d'un côté et de cuivre de l'autre.

Dit gebouw van 93 woningen, dat op een voormalig parkeerterrein staat, maakte deel uit van een renovatieplan voor Barking and Dagenham. De trapsgewijze structuur van de gevel is aan één kant met baksteen bekleed en aan de andere kant met koper.

Whitechapel Dining Room ⑧

77-82 Whitechapel High Street

Project Orange
www.projectorange.com

Photos: © Richard Bryant

Sketch

The expansion of the new restaurant in this prestigious art gallery extends through to part of the adjacent Victorian library. The result is a synthesis between the historic nature of the building and the contemporary artworks on show.

Die Erweiterung des Restaurants dieser renommierten Kunstgalerie schloss einen Teil der benachbarten viktorianischen Bibliothek ein. Entstanden ist ein Stil, in dem der historische Charakter des Bauwerks und die ausgestellten Werke zeitgenössischer Kunst ihren Niederschlag finden.

L'agrandissement du nouveau restaurant de cette prestigieuse galerie d'art est arrivé à une partie de la bibliothèque adjacente de style victorien. Le résultat obtenu est une synthèse entre le caractère historique du bâtiment et les œuvres d'art contemporain qui y sont exposées.

De uitbreiding van het nieuwe restaurant van deze prestigieuze galerie besloeg een deel van de aangrenzende bibliotheek in victoriaanse stijl. Het resultaat is een synthese tussen het historische karakter van het gebouw en de hedendaagse kunstwerken die geëxposeerd worden.

MEET

Shoreditch House ⑨

1 Ebor Street

Tom Dixon / Design Research Studio
www.tomdixon.net

Photos: © Courtesy of Shoreditch House

The interior design of this club located in the old Biscuit Factory pays homage to its industrial past. The eclectic style combines local esthetics with the "British futurism" characteristic to the famous designer commissioned for its transformation.

Die Inneneinrichtung dieses Clubs, der in der ehemaligen Biscuit Factory angesiedelt wurde, macht aus der industriellen Vergangenheit keinen Hehl. Aus lokaler Tradition und dem futuristischen britischen Akzent eines berühmten Designers ergibt sich ein eigenartig eklektischer Stil.

Le design intérieur de ce club installé dans la Biscuit Factory (ancienne fabrique de biscuits) rend hommage à son passé industriel. Le style éclectique marie l'esthétique locale au « futurisme à l'accent britannique », si caractéristique du fameux designer chargé de la transformation.

Het interieur van deze club in de voormalige Biscuit Factory doet het verleden alle eer aan. In de eclectische stijl is plaatselijke esthetiek gecombineerd met 'futurisme met een Brits tintje', dat zo kenmerkend is voor de beroemde ontwerper die het idee heeft vormgegeven.

STAY

Boundary ⑩

2-4 Boundary Street

Conran & Partners
www.conranandpartners.com

Photos: © courtesy of Design Hotels

CAULIFLOWER
£1·80 PER KG
MUSHROOMS

SPROUTS ON THE STEM
£2·80
BABY ONIONS
PENCE
80 KILO

CARROTS
£2·20 PER KILO

CABBAGE
£1·00 EACH

ALBION

ALBION

ALBION

Located in Shoreditch, a fashionable part of East London, each of the 12 rooms in this hotel is dedicated to a designer or an esthetic trend. The rooms and other spaces contain the works of 50 artists, many from the private collection of Terence and Vicki Conran.

In Shoreditch, einem neuerdings beliebten Viertel im Osten Londons, befindet sich dieses Hotel, dessen zwölf Zimmer jeweils einem Designer bzw. einer Kunstrichtung gewidmet sind. Insgesamt sind in den Räumen des Hotels die Werke von 50 Künstlern zu finden; viele von ihnen stammen aus der Privatsammlung von Terence und Vicki Conran.

Situé à Shoreditch, une zone à la mode d'East London, cet hôtel compte douze chambres, chacune consacrée à un designer ou à un courant esthétique. Dans les chambres et le reste des espaces sont exposées les œuvres de 50 artistes, la plupart formant partie de la collection particulière de Terence et Vicki Conran.

Dit hotel staat in de wijk Shoreditch, een centrum van mode in het oosten van Londen. Alle twaalf kamers zijn gewijd aan een ontwerper of esthetische stroming. In het hele gebouw bevinden zich werken van vijftig kunstenaars, waarvan veel afkomstig zijn uit de privécollectie van Terence en Vicki Conran.

LEARN

The Blizard Building 11

4 Newark Street

Alsop Architects
www.alsoparchitects.com

Photos: © Morely von Sternberg

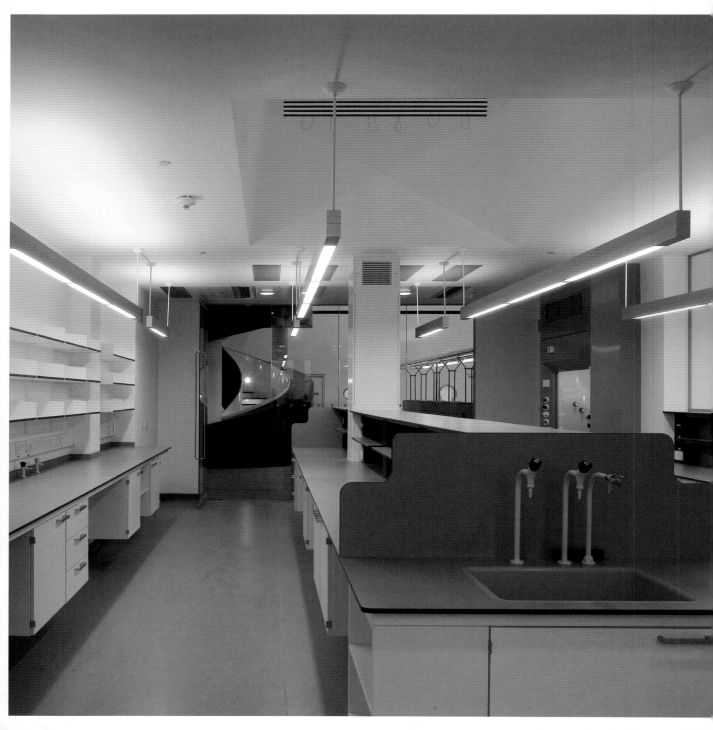

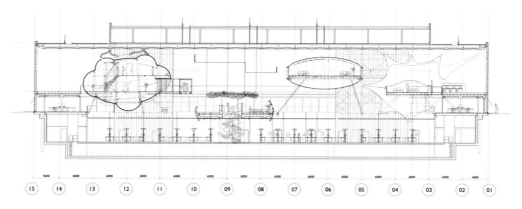

Long section

The University of London's School of Medicine is far removed from conservative laboratory and research center spaces. The rooms and floors are connected by an open space with colored units of biological shapes.

Die medizinische Fakultät der Universität London hat nichts von der einschlägig bekannten Laboratmosphäre solcher Forschungszentren. Die einzelnen Ebenen und Lehrsäle sind über einen offenen Raum miteinander verbunden, der von farbigen, biologisch-dynamischen Formen beherrscht wird.

La faculté de médecine de l'Université de Londres n'a rien des ambiances conservatrices propres aux laboratoires et centres de recherche. Les salles et les étages communiquent par un espace ouvert, avec des parties colorées aux formes biologiques.

De School of Medicine van de University of London doet bepaald niet denken aan een traditioneel laboratorium of onderzoekscentrum. De zalen en verdiepingen zijn met elkaar verbonden in een open ruimte van kleurige, organisch gevormde eenheden.

LEARN

Bridge Academy (12)

Laburnum Street

BDP
www.bdp.com

Photos: © Martine Hamilton

Aerial © Commission Air

Located in a building that had been left to run down in recent years, this school has acted as a regeneration element for the neighborhood. Its shape responds to the desire to maximize natural light in the classrooms.

Dieses Schulgebäude befindet sich in einem in den letzten Jahren vernachlässigten Gebiet und soll die Wiederbelebung der umliegenden Gegend in voranbringen. Seine Form ergibt sich aus dem Wunsch, Bildungsgebäude möglichst mit natürlichem Licht zu versorgen.

Situé dans un bâtiment abandonné ces dernières années, cette école a servi d'élément régénérateur pour le voisinage. Sa forme répond à la volonté d'optimiser l'entrée de lumière naturelle dans les classes.

Dit schoolgebouw staat in een gebied dat de laatste jaren nogal verwaarloosd was en heeft de omgeving nieuw elan gegeven. De vorm van de constructie voldoet aan de wens om zoveel mogelijk daglicht in de lokalen te laten komen.

LEARN

Business School and ⑬ Learning Resource Centre

Dockland Campus, 4–6 University Way

BDP
www.bdp.com

Photos: © David Barbour

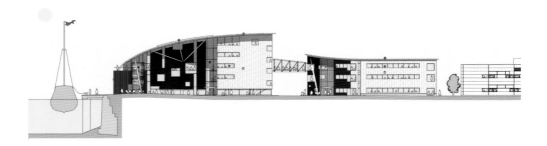

Elevations

This University of East London center comprises two parallel buildings next to the river and joined by a bridge. They look out over the City Airport runways. The interior spaces are large and flexible and visually communicated by the open design of the building.

Dieser Komplex der University of East London besteht aus zwei längs am Fluss stehenden Gebäuden, die durch eine Brücke miteinander verbunden sind. Aus den Gebäuden sieht man auf die Rollbahnen des City Airports. Die Innenräume sind großzügig und flexibel gestaltet und dank des offenen Gestaltungskonzepts visuell nicht voneinander getrennt.

Ce centre de l'Université d'East London compte deux bâtiments parallèles à la rivière et reliés par un pont. Les constructions font face aux pistes de l'aéroport de la City. Les espaces intérieurs sont généreux et modulables, et visuellement communiqués grâce au design ouvert de l'ensemble.

Dit centrum van de University of East London bestaat uit twee gebouwen die parallel aan de rivier staan en door een brug met elkaar verbonden zijn. De bouwwerken kijken uit op de landingsbanen van London City Airport. De ruimten binnen zijn ruim en flexibel, en vormen een eenheid dankzij het open ontwerp.

CREATE

Rich Mix (14)

35 Bethnal Green Road

Penoyre & Prasad
www.penoyre-prasad.net

Photos: © Morley Von Sternberg; Chris Gascoigne/VIEW

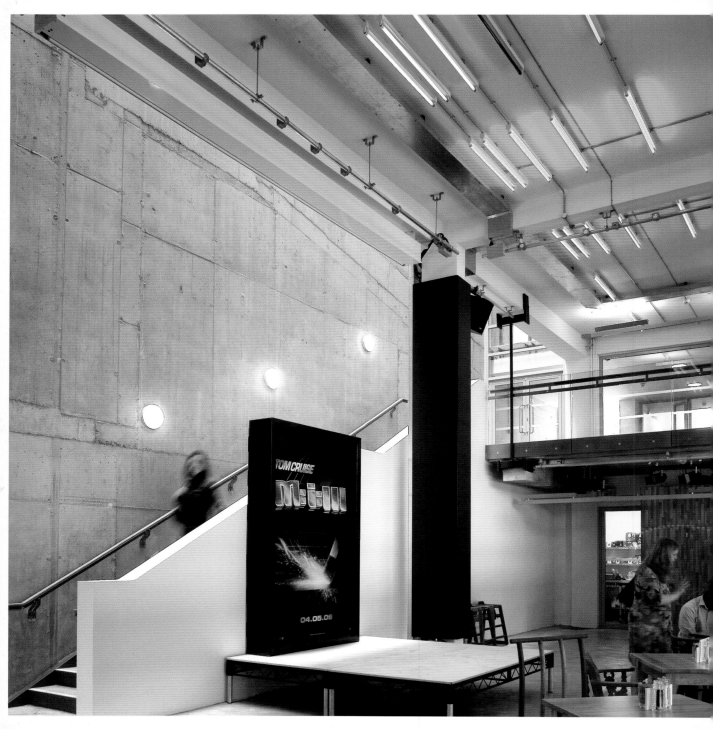

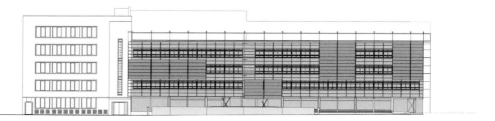

Elevation

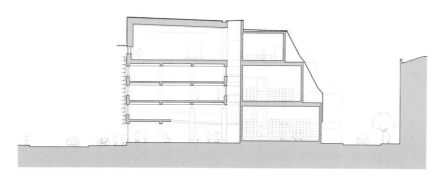

Section

This cultural center includes the renovation of a former leather-goods warehouse along with new facilities. It boasts cinemas and exhibition and events rooms. The façade is a dynamic element with a constantly changing appearance thanks to the use of metal fillets.

Eine ehemalige Lederwarenfabrik wurde zu einem Kulturzentrum umgebaut und durch Kinosäle, Ausstellungs- und Veranstaltungsräume erweitert. Die Fassade stellt sich dank der verwendeten Metallprofile als dynamisches, sich ständig veränderndes Element dar.

Ce centre culturel compte une partie rénovée d'anciens ateliers de maroquinerie et de nouvelles installations, dont des cinémas et des salles d'expositions et de spectacles. La façade est un élément dynamique dont l'apparence change constamment grâce aux baguettes métalliques qui la composent.

Een deel van dit cultureel centrum bestaat uit een voormalige, verbouwde lederwarenwerkplaats. Daarnaast zijn er nieuwe voorzieningen gebouwd zoals bioscopen, tentoonstellingsruimten en theaters. De gevel is een dynamisch element, dat dankzij de metalen platen voortdurend van uiterlijk verandert.

LIVE

Bacon Street (15)

30 Bacon Street

Pentagram
www.pentagram.com

Photos: © Ed Reeve

The result of a radical overhaul, this house in Brick Lane is the home of one of the architects behind Pentagram. The cement and glass building contrasts with the brick structures that predominate in this fashionable East London neighborhood.

Mitten in der Brick Lane steht dieses Haus, in dem Architekten des Büros Pentagram wohnen. Es wurde von Grund auf umgebaut und bildet mit Beton und Glas als Baumaterial einen lebhaften Kontrast zu den Backsteinbauten der Umgebung im Osten Londons.

Fruit d'une rénovation radicale, cette maison en plein cœur de Brick Lane est le logement de l'un des architectes de Pentagram. La construction en ciment et verre contraste avec celles en briques si courantes dans le quartier en vogue d'East London.

Dit radicaal verbouwde huis midden in Brick Lane is de woning van architecten van Pentagram. De constructie van cement en glas contrasteert met de bakstenen gebouwen die deze modewijk in het oosten van Londen domineren.

WORK

Hiltongrove (16)

10-15 Hatheley Mews

Friend and Company
www.friendandcompany.co.uk

Photos: © David Cowlard/Urban Exposure

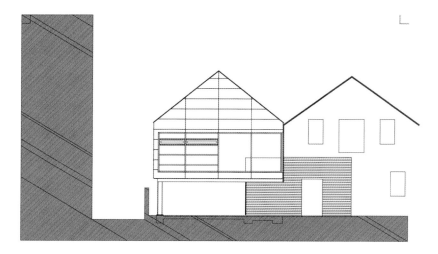

Elevation

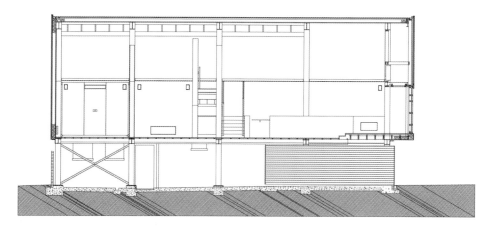

Section

The projecting façade of this building which houses the offices of a music company stands out from the neighboring buildings. Inside, the light-bathed large central space contains a mezzanine level that generates a suspended volume.

Die auskragende Fassade dieses Gebäudes, in dem die Büroräume eines Musikverlages untergebracht sind, hebt sich von der Bebauung der Umgebung ab. Im lichtdurchfluteten zentralen Innenraum sticht ein Zwischengeschoss ins Auge, das zu schweben scheint.

La façade en saillie de ce bâtiment qui accueille les bureaux d'une compagnie musicale se démarque des constructions voisines. À l'intérieur, le généreux espace central baigné de lumière inclut un entresol dégageant un volume suspendu.

De uitstekende gevel van dit gebouw waarin een muziekvereniging is gehuisvest, valt erg op tussen de andere constructies in de omgeving. De grote centrale ruimte binnen krijgt overvloedig daglicht en heeft een tussenverdieping die een hangend volume creëert.

WEST

The Royal Borough of Kensington
and Chelsea
PORTOBELLO
ROAD, W.11.

FRESH COCONUT WATER!! DELICIOUS & NUTRITIOUS

FRESH COCONUT WATER

SAUSAGE & ALE TASTING MONDAYS FROM 6 PM

SEE

Saatchi Gallery ①

Duke of York's HQ, King's Road

Allford Hall Monaghan Morris
www.ahmm.co.uk

Photos: © Timothy Soar

The new gallery covers over 67,000 sq ft of the Victorian building known as the Duke of York's Headquarters. The new facilities take advantage of the original architecture and include new exhibition spaces and a simple circulation system.

Die neue Galerie nimmt fast 6.200 Quadratmeter des viktorianischen Gebäudes ein, das als The Duke of York's Headquarters bekannt ist. Die neuen Räumlichkeiten nutzen die Vorteile des Altbaus und umfassen neue Ausstellungsflächen sowie ein einfaches Erschließungssystem.

La nouvelle galerie occupe près de 6 200 m^2 du bâtiment victorien connu comme Duke of York's Headquarters. Les nouvelles installations profitent de l'architecture d'origine et intègrent de nouveaux espaces d'exposition et un système simple de circulation.

De nieuwe Gallery beslaat bijna 6200 vierkante meter van het victoriaanse gebouw dat bekendstaat als The Duke of York's Headquarters. Bij de nieuwe installaties is geprofiteerd van de oorspronkelijke architectuur. Er zijn o.a. nieuwe tentoonstellingsruimten en een eenvoudig circulatiesysteem gekomen.

STROLL

Serpentine Gallery Pavilion ②

Kensington Gardens

Oscar Niemeyer; Alvaro Siza and Eduardo Souto Moura;
Rem Koolhaas and Cecil Balmond; Frank Gehry;
Olafur Eliasson and Kjetil Thorsen

Photos: © John Offenbach, Richard Bryant/arcaid.co.uk

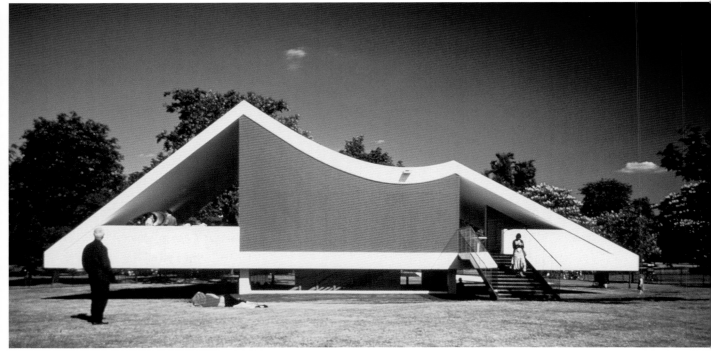

Each year the Serpentine Gallery selects a team of internationally renowned architects to design a pavilion in Kensington Gardens, as a small hands-on demonstration of contemporary architecture.

Jedes Jahr wählt die Serpentine Gallery ein international renommiertes Architektenteam aus, das dann einen Pavillon in den Kensington Gardens entwirft und damit ein praktisches Beispiel zeitgenössischer Architektur vorstellt.

Chaque année, la Serpentine Gallery sélectionne une équipe d'architectes de renommée internationale pour concevoir un pavillon dans les Kensington Gardens, tel un petit échantillon pratique d'architecture contemporaine.

Elk jaar kiest de Serpentine Gallery een architectenbureau van internationale faam om een paviljoen in Kensington Gardens te ontwerpen, als een klein praktijkvoorbeeld van hedendaagse architectuur.

TASTE

Artisan du Chocolat ③

81 Westbourne Grove

Lens°Ass architecten
www.lensass.be

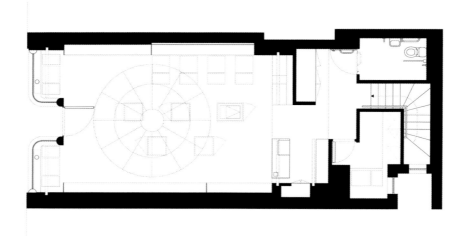

Floor plan

The panoramic photo of a cocoa plantation printed inside the XXXL lamp by Bart Lens is the center of attention in this chocolate store. The size of the lamp generates a 'space inside a space' which contrasts with the rest of the flat surfaces.

Ein Panoramafoto einer Kakaoplantage, das auf der Lampe XXXL von Bart Lens gedruckt erscheint, bildet den Blickfang dieses Schokoladengeschäfts. Die Dimensionen dieser Installation schaffen einen Raum im Raum, der mit den übrigen glatten Oberflächen kontrastiert.

La photo panoramique d'une plantation de cacao imprimée à l'intérieur de la lampe « XXXL » de Bart Lens est le point de mire dans ce magasin de chocolats. Les dimensions de l'objet créent un espace dans l'espace tranchant avec le reste des surfaces planes.

De blikvanger van deze chocoladewinkel is de panoramische foto van een cacaoplantage die op de binnenkant van een XXXL-lamp van Bart Lens gedrukt is. Door de afmetingen van het object ontstaat een ruimte binnen de ruimte, die contrasteert met de overige gladde oppervlakken.

WORK

Engine offices (4)

60 Great Portland Street

Jump Studios
www.jump-studios.com

Photos: © Gareth Gardner, Mike Torrington

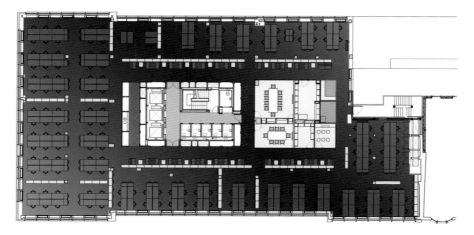

First floor plan

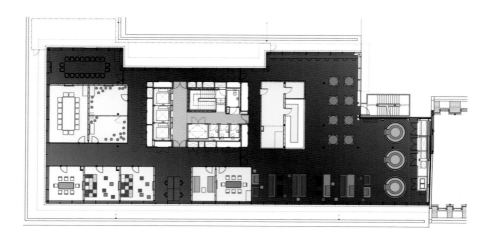

Ground floor plan

The offices of communication group Engine are fitted with elements of highly defined shapes. One of the most impressive is the floating auditorium in the entrance, designed for presentations, and the circular cabins where you can enjoy a coffee while looking out over the city.

Das Verwaltungsgebäude des Medienunternehmens Engine ist mit interessanten Elementen verschiedenster Art ausgestattet. Zu den originellsten gehören der schwebende Vorführraum am Eingang und die runden Kabinen, aus denen man beim Kaffeetrinken den Blick über die Stadt genießen kann.

Les bureaux du groupe de communication Engine sont dotés d'éléments aux formes très marquées. Parmi les plus significatifs, l'auditorium flottant de l'entrée a été conçu pour les présentations et les cabines circulaires permettent de savourer un café tout en profitant des vues de la ville.

Het kantoor van The Engine Group is opgebouwd uit elementen met een uitgesproken vorm. Het opvallendst zijn het zwevende auditorium bij de ingang, bedoeld voor voorstellingen, en de ronde cabines waar je bij een kopje koffie van het uitzicht kunt genieten.

LIVE

100 West Cromwell Road ⑤

Kensington

Bolles+Wilson
www.bolles-wilson.com

Model images © Julian Vogt
All other images: Bolles+Wilson

The pleasingly rounded shape of this building will echo the curves of the street. The windows will form an 'E' shape starting from the third floor above the northern face. Opposite, the full-glass façade will afford views over the winter gardens.

Die abgerundete Form dieses Hochhauses ergibt sich aus der kurvigen Straßenführung. An der Nordseite bilden die Fenster ab der dritten Etage ein großes „E". Auf der gegenüber liegenden Seite fällt der Blick durch die vollständig verglaste Fassade auf einen Wintergarten.

La forme arrondie de ce bâtiment fera écho aux courbes de la rue. Les fenêtres dessineront une silhouette en « E » à partir du troisième étage, sur la face nord. À l'opposé, la façade entièrement vitrée permettra d'apprécier les jardins d'hiver.

De gedraaide vorm van deze toren correspondeert met de bochten in de straat. Aan de noordzijde vormen de ramen vanaf de derde verdieping een E. Daartegenover zijn door de geheel glazen gevel de wintertuinen te zien.

WORK

The Yellow Building 6

Notting Dale Village

Allford Hall Monaghan Morris
www.ahmm.co.uk

Photos: © Timothy Soar

The main office of fashion business Monsoon Accesorize is a 160,000-sq-ft building that houses offices and design studios as well as various real-scale models of the chain's establishments. A central atrium runs the length of the seven floors, crossed by bridges and a large open staircase.

Der Hauptsitz des Modehauses Monsoon Accesorize umfasst 15.000 Quadratmeter Nutzfläche. Das Gebäude enthält Büroräume und Designerstudios sowie eine ganze Reihe von Nachbildungen der Ladengeschäfte des Unternehmens in Originalgröße. Das zentrale Atrium reicht über sieben Geschosse und wird von Brücken und einer großen Freitreppe durchkreuzt.

Le siège social de la marque de mode Monsoon Accesorize occupe un bâtiment de 15 000 m^2. La construction renferme des bureaux et des studios de design, ainsi que plusieurs maquettes à échelle réelle de magasins de la marque. Au centre, une cour intérieure se dresse sur les sept étages et est traversée par des ponts et un grand escalier ouvert.

Het hoofdkantoor van modehuis Monsoon Accesorize is een gebouw van 15.000 vierkante meter. Het huisvest kantoren en ontwerpstudio's, en diverse maquettes van winkels van het merk op ware grootte. Het centrale atrium reikt tot alle zeven verdiepingen en wordt doorsneden door bruggen en een grote open trap.

WORK

Adshel and Clear Channel ⑦

Cromwell Road

Pentagram
www.pentagram.com

Photos: © Nick Turner, Tim Soar, Phil Sayer

Model

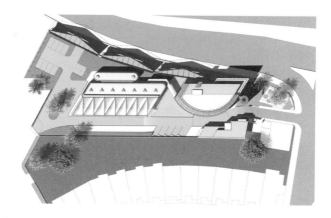

Site plan

A new five-story semicircular building is home to Clear Channel's Center for Design and Research, adjacent to the building of the associated firm Adshel. The buildings are functionally and esthetically complemented with this campus.

Ein fünfgeschossiger Neubau über halbkreisförmigem Grundriss nimmt das Design- und Forschungszentrum von Clear Channel auf. Nebenan befinden sich die Einrichtungen des zur selben Gruppe gehörenden Unternehmens Adshel. Die beiden Gebäude ergänzen sich in funktioneller und ästhetischer Hinsicht.

Un nouveau bâtiment de cinq étages en forme de demi-cercle héberge le centre de design et de recherche de Clear Chanel, adjacent à son partenaire Adshel. Grâce à ce complexe, les deux bâtiments se complètent sur le plan fonctionnel et esthétique.

In een nieuw gebouw van vijf verdiepingen in de vorm van een halve cirkel zijn het ontwerp- en onderzoekscentrum van Clear Chanel ondergebracht, naast het bijbehorende bedrijf Adshel. Met deze campus vullen beide gebouwen elkaar functioneel en esthetisch aan.

READ

The London Library ⑧

14 St James Square

Haworth Tompkins
www.haworthtompkins.com

Photos: © Paul Raftery, Haworth Tompkins

KEEP CLEAR

2

☞

BOOKSTACKS

OFFICES

Acquisitions

Cataloguing

Renderings

Since its foundation in 1841, this independent reference library has been annexing neighboring buildings. The alterations following the latest acquisition use a contemporary but discreet architectural language that respects the character of the original buildings.

Seit ihrer Gründung im Jahre 1841 ist diese unabhängige Bibliothek immer wieder um angrenzende Gebäude erweitert worden. Die letzte Erweiterung gab Anlass zu einem Umbau in zeitgenössischer Formensprache, dessen diskreter Charakter den Charme der älteren Gebäudeteile jedoch nicht mindert.

Depuis sa fondation en 1841, cette bibliothèque indépendante de référence a intégré des bâtiments annexes. Les modifications effectuées après la dernière acquisition font appel à un langage architectonique contemporain mais discret, dans le respect du caractère des bâtiments d'origine.

Sinds de oprichting in 1841 heeft deze onafhankelijke bibliotheek er voortdurend aangrenzende gebouwen bij gekregen. Bij de renovatie van de laatste aanwinst is een hedendaagse, maar ingetogen architectonische taal gebruikt, die het karakter van de oorspronkelijke gebouwen respecteert.

EAT

Olivomare ⑨

10 Lower Belgrave Street

Pierluigi Piu
www.pierluigipiu.it

Photos: © courtesy of Olivomare

Olivomare is a seafood restaurant whose decor boasts references to the marine world. The pattern on the large main wall is inspired by the etchings of Maurits Escher.

Olivomare ist der Name dieses Restaurants, dessen Spezialität Meeresfrüchte sind. Dementsprechend wurden die Räume mit maritimen Motiven ausgeschmückt. Die Gestaltung der Längswand greift auf eine Zeichnung von Maurits Escher zurück.

Olivomare est un restaurant de fruits de mer, d'où les nombreuses références au monde marin dans sa décoration. Le motif du grand mur principal s'est inspiré des dessins de Maurits Escher.

Olivomare is een in zeevruchten gespecialiseerd restaurant. De inrichting heeft veel verwijzingen naar de wereld van de zee. De print op de grote wand is geïnspireerd op de tekeningen van M.C. Escher.

DISCOVER

The Darwin Centre ⑩

Natural History Museum, Cromwell Road

C. F. Møller Architects
www.cfmoller.com

Photos: © Torben Eskerod

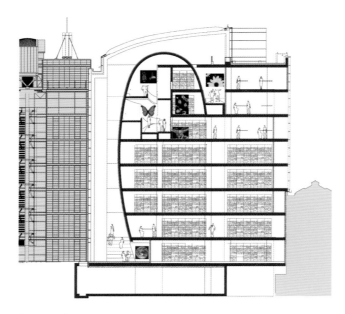

Cross section

Long section

The design of the second phase of the Natural History Museum's Darwin Centre resulted in a cocoon-shaped structure that houses the museum's entomological and botanical specimens. Its scale is such that it cannot be seen in its entirety from any position.

Für die zweite Phase des Darwin Zentrums des Museums für Naturgeschichte, wurde als Heim für die entomologischen und botanischen Sammlungen ein Entwurf ausgewählt, der an eine Knospe erinnert. Aufgrund seiner Größe kann dieses Gebäude von keinem Standpunkt aus vollständig erfasst/eingesehen werden.

Le design de la seconde phase du Darwin Centre, dans le Muséum d'histoire naturelle, a donné une structure en forme de cocon pour accueillir les spécimens entomologiques et botaniques. Sa taille est telle qu'il est impossible de l'apprécier dans sa totalité.

Het ontwerp van de tweede fase van het Darwin Centre van het Museum of Natural History werd een structuur met een coconvorm, waarin de entomologische en botanische collecties zijn ondergebracht. Hij is zo groot dat hij vanuit geen enkele positie in zijn geheel te zien is.

NORTH

HEAL

Kentish Town Health Centre ①

2 Bartholomew Rd

Allford Hall Monaghan Morris
www.ahmm.co.uk

Photos: © Timothy Soar

This health center building was designed using concepts of transparency, innovation and connectivity. The double- and triple-height central courtyard is crossed by bridges and balconies and boasts colored graphics and a bright signaling system designed by Studio Myerscough.

Transparenz, Innovation und kurze Wege waren die Vorgaben beim Entwurf dieses Gesundheitszentrums. Der über zwei bzw. drei Geschosse reichende Innenhof wird von Stegen, Balkonen und Schriftzügen durchkreuzt und von dem auffälligen Leitsystem des Büros Myerscough genutzt.

Le bâtiment de ce centre médical a été pensé en termes de transparence, d'innovation et de connectivité. La cour centrale de double et triple hauteur est traversée par des ponts et des balcons. Elle montre des graphiques de couleur et un système flambant de signalisation conçu par Studio Myerscough.

Dit gezondheidscentrum werd ontworpen rond de concepten transparantie, innovatie en verbinding. In de centrale hal van dubbele en driedubbele hoogte wordt de ruimte gebroken door bruggen, balkons en kleurige vormen. De opvallende bewegwijzering is ontworpen door Studio Myerscough.

LIVE

44-45 Newington Green ②

Islington

Haworth Tompkins
www.haworthtompkins.com

Photos: © Philip Vile; Haworth Tompins; Fisher Hart; Lukasz Kowalski

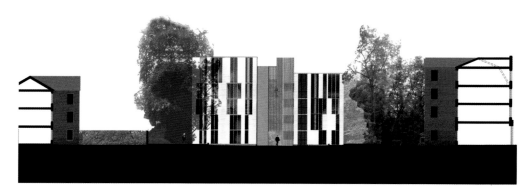

Elevation

The building, with 200 rooms for City University students, is the result of the remodeling of one existing building and the substitution of another for completely new blocks and spaces for gardens.

Zur Schaffung von 200 Zimmern für die Studenten der City University wurde ein bestehendes Gebäude vollständig umgebaut und ein weiteres anstelle eines Altbaus neu errichtet. Außerdem wurden die Außenanlagen begrünt.

Avec 200 chambres pour les étudiants de l'Université de la City, le bâtiment est le fruit de la rénovation d'une construction existante et en remplace une autre par des blocs entièrement nouveaux et des espaces verts.

Dit gebouw telt 200 kamers voor studenten van de City University. Het is deels het resultaat van de renovatie van bestaande bouw. De volledig nieuwe blokken en de tuinruimten zijn in de plaats gekomen van een ander gebouw.

LIVE

Camden House ③

Grafton Crescent

Crawford Partnership
www.crawfordpartnership.co.uk

Photos: © James Tye

Elevations

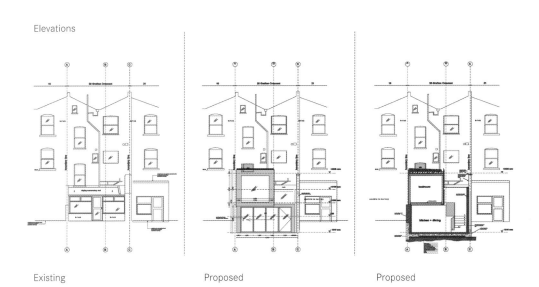

Existing   Proposed   Proposed

The renovation of this traditional home consists of the expansion of the ground-floor kitchen/dining room and a wooden cube above which acts as a multi-purpose space.

Der Umbau dieses traditionellen Wohnhauses umfasste die Erweiterung der Küche mit anschließendem Esszimmer im Erdgeschoss und den Bau eines Holzwürfels im oberen Teil, der als eigenständige Wohneinheit fungiert.

La rénovation de ce logement traditionnel inclut l'agrandissement de la cuisine/salle à manger au bas, ainsi qu'un cube en bois à l'étage en guise de pièce polyvalente.

De renovatie van deze traditionele woning bestaat uit een uitbreiding van de keuken annex eetkamer op de begane grond en de bouw van een houten kubus op de bovenverdieping die dienst doet als multifunctioneel vertrek.

LIVE

Lambolle Place ④

7 Lambolle Place

Andy Martin Associates
www.andymartinassociates.com

Photos: © Nick Rochowski

Plans and sections

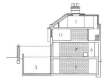

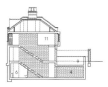

Roof plan

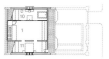
Second floor plan

First floor plan

Ground floor plan

Basement plan

1 Living
2 Office
3 Courtyard
4 Plant/utilities
5 WC
6 Kitchen
7 Dining
8 Car space
9 Pond
10 Bathroom
11 Bedroom

An old garage was turned into a four-story home for the family of a musician and his designer wife. Plays of light and shadow and contrasts between white and black are constant features throughout.

Eine ehemalige Garage wurde zu einem viergeschossigen Wohnhaus umgebaut, in dem nun ein Musiker und eine Designerin mit ihren Kindern leben. Das Motiv des Licht- und Schattenspiels, der Schwarz-Weiß-Kontrast, zieht sich durch alle Räume des Hauses.

Un ancien garage a été converti en logement de quatre étages pour la famille d'un musicien et de sa femme designer. Les jeux de lumière et d'ombres et les contrastes noir/blanc sont une constante à travers toute la maison.

Van een voormalige garage is een woning van vier verdiepingen gemaakt voor een gezin waarin de man musicus en de vrouw ontwerpster is. Het spel van licht en schaduw en het contrast tussen wit en zwart komen steeds terug in alle ruimten van het huis.

SOUTH

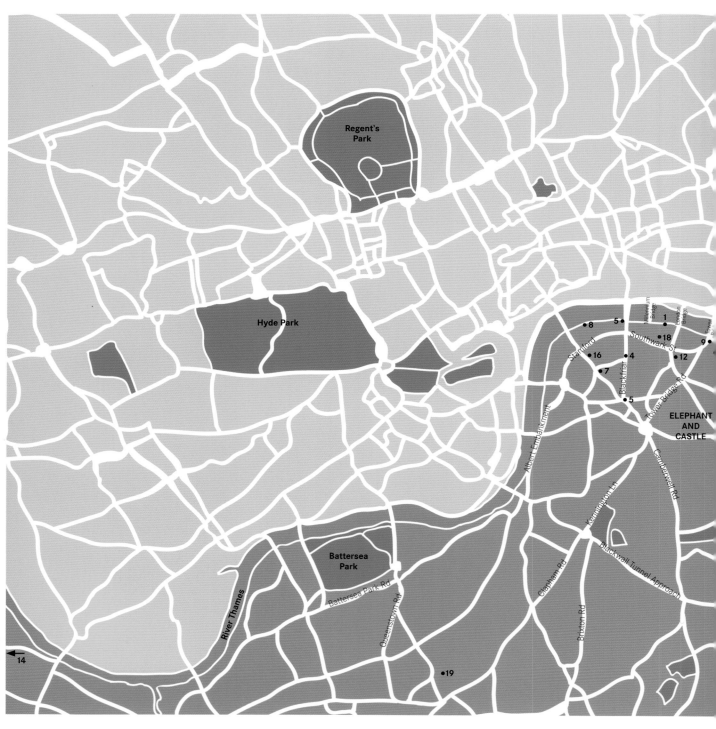

RULE

City Hall ①

110 The Queens Walk

Foster and Partners
www.fosterandpartners.com

Photos: © Foster + Partners

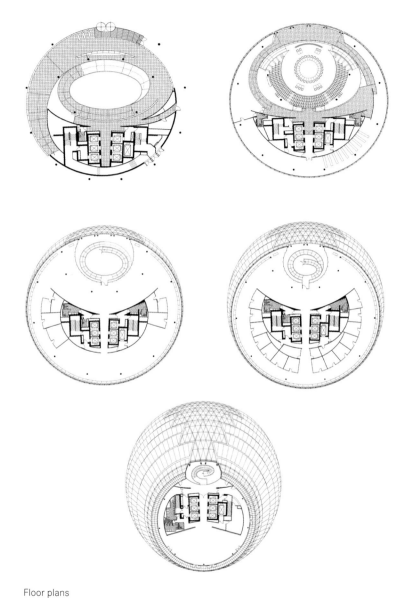

Floor plans

This oval-shaped building has a transparent structure that is a nod to the democratic processes it houses as the seat of local government. The orientation allows the sustainable behavior of the structure.

Die transparente Struktur dieses ovalen Gebäudes spielt auf das demokratische Gemeinwesen an, denn es ist Sitz der Stadtregierung. Seine Orientierung folgt den Vorgaben der Umweltverträglichkeit.

Ce bâtiment de forme ovale possède une structure transparente en hommage aux processus démocratiques dont il est le théâtre en tant que siège du gouvernement local. L'orientation favorise le comportement durable de la structure.

Dit ovale gebouw, de zetel van het stadsbestuur, heeft een transparante structuur die verwijst naar de democratische processen die er plaatsvinden. Dankzij de oriëntatie van het gebouw is er sprake van een milieuvriendelijke constructie.

LEARN

Ben Pimlott Building ②

New Cross

Alsop Architects
www.alsoparchitects.com

Photos: © Roderick Coyne

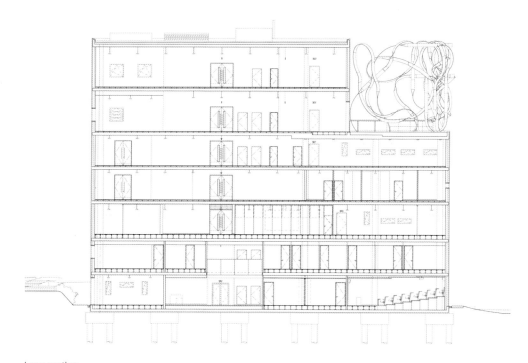

Long section

This building houses Goldsmiths, University of London, studios and resembles a steel box. Three of the four faces are clad in metal, while the full-glass north façade allows abundant natural light in.

Das Gebäude der Studiensäle des Goldsmith College der Universität London sieht aus wie eine große stählerne Kiste. Drei Seiten sind mit Metallpaneelen verkleidet, während die Nordfassade vo llständig verglast ist und so das Tageslicht ungehindert ins Innere fluten lässt.

Ce bâtiment de l'université Goldsmiths de Londres s'apparente à une caisse en acier. Trois des quatre faces sont revêtues de métal, alors que la façade nord est entièrement vitrée pour laisser pénétrer l'abondante lumière naturelle.

Dit gebouw van het Goldsmiths College van de University of London waarin studio's zijn gehuisvest, lijkt op een stalen kist. Drie van de vier gevels zijn met metaal bekleed. Door de noordelijke gevel, die geheel uit glas bestaat, stroomt het daglicht rijkelijk binnen.

WORK

Palestra ③

197 Blackfriars Road

Alsop Architects
www.alsoparchitects.com

Photos: © Christian Richters

197
Blackfriars
Road

Sketch

This building is home to the offices of investment companies and comprises three volumes piled on top of each other. The ground-floor structure lifts the building nearly 20 feet westward to create a dynamic entrance. The upper and lower boxes are differentiated by shape and color.

In diesem Gebäude sind mehrere Investmentgesellschaften untergebracht. Die Struktur ist in drei aufeinander gestapelte Module unterteilt. Der unterste Block ist gegen Westen sechs Meter über das Straßenniveau angehoben, um den Eingangsbereich dynamischer zu gestalten. Die beiden anderen Blöcke heben sich durch ihre Farbgebung ab.

Ce bâtiment, qui héberge les bureaux de compagnies d'investissements, se compose de trois volumes empilés. Le corps au niveau du sol dresse l'ensemble sur 6 mètres vers l'ouest pour dégager une entrée dynamique. Les blocs supérieurs et inférieurs se distinguent par leur forme et leur couleur.

Dit gebouw dat kantoren van investeringsmaatschappijen huisvest, bestaat uit drie boven elkaar geplaatste volumes. Het volume op de begane grond laat het gebouw zo'n 6 meter in westelijke richting omhoogkomen en creëert zo een dynamische ingang. De onderste en bovenste volumes zijn anders van vorm en kleur.

LIVE

One Blackfriars Road (4)

Southwark

Ian Simpson Architects
www.iansimpsonarchitects.com

Drawings: © Ian Simpson Architects

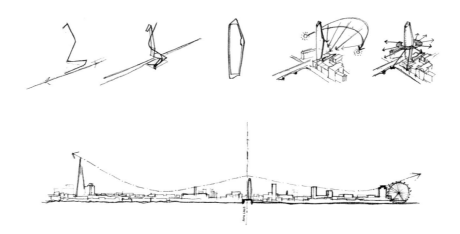

Sketches

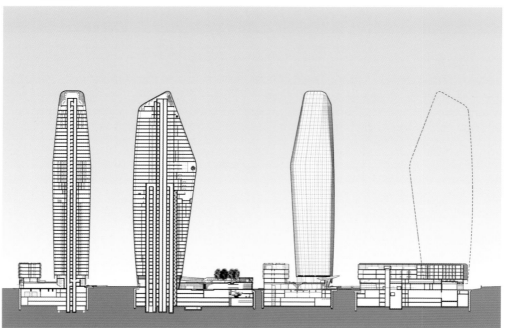

Sections

The construction that will house a five-star hotel and luxury apartments is set to change the London skyline upon completion in 2014. It comprises a two-floor base with a 55-foot tower in the northeast sector and a further six floors on the western corner of the site.

Wenn dieses Hochhaus im Jahre 2014 vollendet ist, wird es die Skyline Londons entscheidend verändern. Der Komplex umfasst einen zweigeschossigen Sockelbau, einen 170 Meter hohen Turm im Nordosten sowie einen sechsstöckigen Bau in der Westecke und soll ein 5-Sterne-Hotel und Luxusappartements aufnehmen.

La construction, qui accueillera un hôtel cinq étoiles et des appartements de luxe, changera le skyline de Londres une fois terminée en 2014. La base de deux étages compte une tour de 170 mètres de haut dans le secteur nord-est et une autre de 6 étages dans l'angle ouest de l'ensemble.

Dit bouwwerk, dat een vijfsterrenhotel en luxeappartementen huisvest, zal na zijn voltooiing in 2014 de skyline van Londen drastisch veranderen. Het heeft een basis van twee verdiepingen en een toren van 170 meter hoog in het noordwestelijke deel en een van zes verdiepingen op de westelijke hoek.

LIVE

The London Bridge Tower ⑤

Adjacent to London Bridge Station
32 London Bridge St

Renzo Piano Building Workshop
rpbw.r.ui-pro.com

Drawings: © Renzo Piano Building Workshop

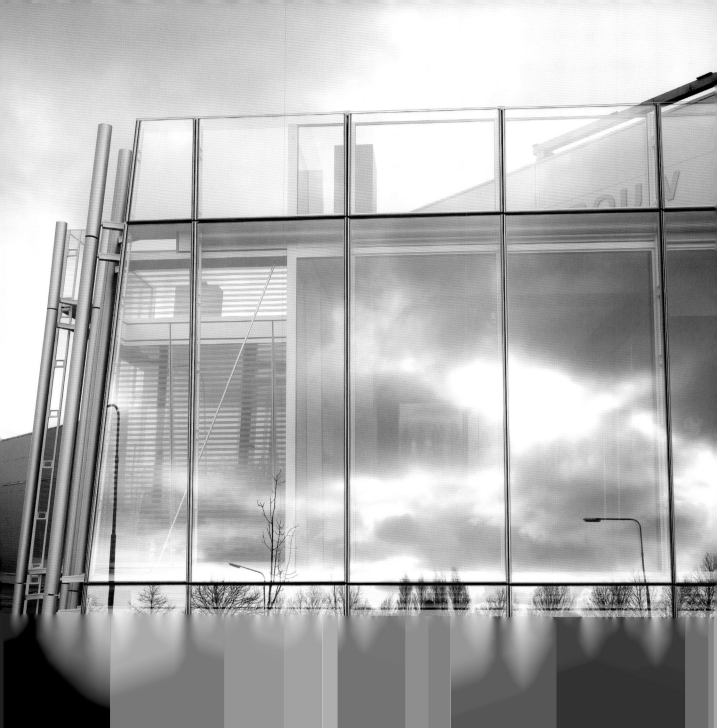

Sketch

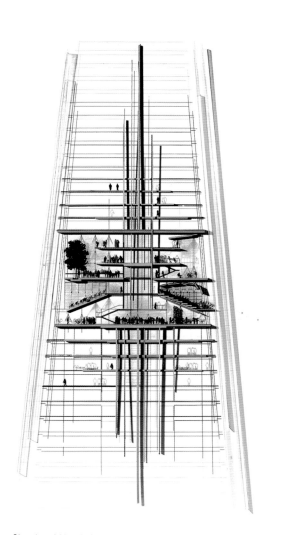

Sketch: mid level piazza and façade

This building, which will stand over 1,000 feet tall, was designed as a glass pyramid. Each façade forms a fragment, an inclined glass sheet that dissolves as it reaches the apex. The corners are open and the sheets of glass do not touch each other.

Dieser Wolkenkratzer wird 306 Meter hoch sein und die Form einer gläsernen Pyramide haben. Jede Fassade bildet dabei eine schräge Fläche aus Glas, die sich zur Spitze hin auflöst. Die Grate sind offen konzipiert, sodass die Glasflächen einander dort nicht berühren.

S'élevant sur plus de 300 mètres, ce bâtiment a été conçu comme une pyramide vitrée. Chaque façade forme un fragment, un plan en verre incliné qui se termine au sommet. Les angles sont ouverts et les plaques en verre ne sont pas en contact.

Dit gebouw, dat 306 meter hoog wordt, is ontworpen als een piramide van glas. Elke zijde vormt een fragment, een hellend vlak van glas dat in de top oplost. De hoeken zijn open en de glazen platen raken elkaar niet.

SEE

Young Vic Theatre 6

66 The Cut

Haworth Tompkins
www.haworthtompkins.com

Photos: © Philip Vile; Haworth Tompkins

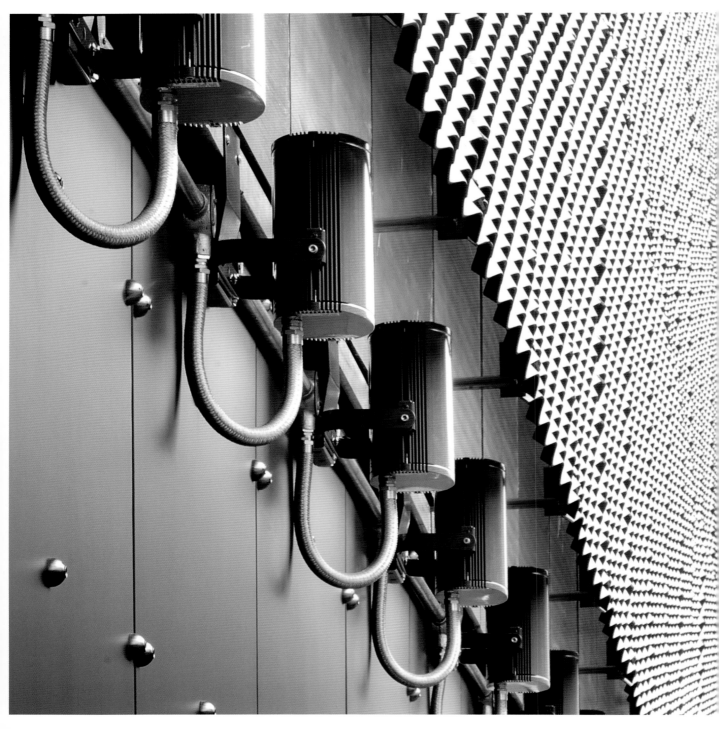

The renovation of this enigmatic London theater included alterations to the auditorium and the addition of two new studios along with offices, works spaces and a new foyer. The design arose from conversations with local artists, theater employees and local residents.

Die Renovierung dieses verwunschenen Londoner Theaters umfasste den Umbau des Zuschauerraums, die Schaffung zweier neuer Probensäle, neuer Büros und Arbeitsräume sowie eines neuen Foyers. Die Gestaltung wurde mit ortsansässigen Künstlern, den Mitarbeitern des Theaters und den Nachbarn abgesprochen.

La rénovation de cet énigmatique théâtre londonien a inclus la restauration de l'auditorium et l'ajout de deux nouveaux studios, des bureaux, des espaces de travail et un nouveau foyer. Le design s'est élaboré au fil des conversations avec les artistes locaux, les employés du théâtre et les voisins.

Bij de renovatie van dit mysterieuze Londense theater werd de theaterzaal verbouwd en kwamen er twee nieuwe studio's, kantoren en werkruimten, en een nieuwe foyer. Aan de hand van gesprekken met buren, artiesten en andere mensen die werkzaam waren in het theater werd het ontwerp ontwikkeld.

REHEARSE

The Royal National Theatre Studio (7)

South Bank

Haworth Tompkins
www.haworthtompkins.com

Photos: © Philip Vile; Haworth Tompkins

The 1958 building protected as an example of the New Brutalism style was remodeled to house rehearsal rooms, a public archive and offices for National Theatre scriptwriters.

Das Gebäude aus dem Jahre 1958 steht als Beispiel des „Brutalismus" unter Denkmalschutz. Es wurde umgebaut, um zwei Probensäle, ein öffentliches Archiv und die Büroräume der Drehbuchautoren des National Theatre aufzunehmen.

Le bâtiment de 1958 protégé, échantillon du style Nouveau Brutalisme, a été rénové pour accueillir deux salles de répétitions, une archive publique et des bureaux pour les scénaristes National Theater.

Dit gebouw uit 1958 is beschermd omdat het een voorbeeld is van het brutalisme in de architectuur. Het werd gerenoveerd om ruimte te bieden aan twee repetitieruimten, een openbaar archief en kantoren voor scenarioschrijvers van het National Theatre.

SEE

Unicorn Theatre 8

147 Tooley Street

Keith Williams Architects
www.keithwilliamsarchitects.com

Photos: © Hélène Binet

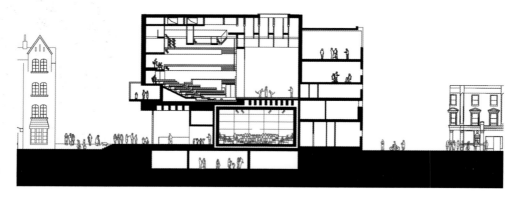

Section

This children's theater was designed as an asymmetrical pavilion. The transparent façade surfaces allow views into the various levels of the foyer that lead to the Studio Theatre and the main auditorium.

In diesem Theater werden Stücke für Kinder aufgeführt. Der Entwurf sah einen asymmetrischen Pavillon vor. Die durchsichtigen Oberflächen der Fassade lassen die verschiedenen Ebenen des Foyers erkennen, die vor dem Studio Theatre bzw. dem großen Vorführsaal liegen.

Ce théâtre pour enfants a été conçu comme un pavillon asymétrique. Les surfaces transparentes de la façade révèlent les divers niveaux du foyer menant au Studio Theatre et à l'auditorium principal.

Dit theater, dat gespecialiseerd is in kindervoorstellingen, is ontworpen als een asymmetrisch paviljoen. Door de transparante vlakken in de gevel zijn de vele niveaus van de foyer te zien, die naar het Studio Theatre en de grote zaal leiden.

SEE

National Maritime Museum, ⑨ South West Wing Project

Romney Road

C. F. Møller Architects
www.cfmoller.com

Drawings: © C. F. Møller Architects

The National Maritime Museum will have a new wing to house a 10,000-sq-ft gallery for special exhibitions, a new entrance from Greenwich Park and research and teaching facilities from the National Maritime Archive.

Das Marinemuseum in Greenwich erhält einen Anbau, der eine Galerie mit 1.000 Quadratmetern Ausstellungsfläche für Sonderschauen aufnimmt, ein neues Eingangstor vom Greenwich Park aus vorsieht und dem Nationalen Marinearchiv Räume für Forschung und Museumspädagogik zur Verfügung stellt.

Le Musée national de la Marine possédera une nouvelle aile qui accueillera une grande galerie de mille mètres carrés pour des expositions temporaires, un nouvel accès depuis le parc de Greenwich et des installations pour la recherche et l'enseignement des archives de la Marine nationale.

Het National Maritime Museum krijgt een nieuwe vleugel waarin een grote zaal van 1.000 vierkante meter voor bijzondere exposities zal worden ondergebracht. Tevens komt er een nieuwe ingang die vanuit Greenwich Park te bereiken is, en faciliteiten voor onderzoek voor het National Maritime Archive.

DANCE

Matter 10

Drawdock Road

Pentagram
www.pentagram.com www.pentagram.com

Photos: © Gavin Jackson

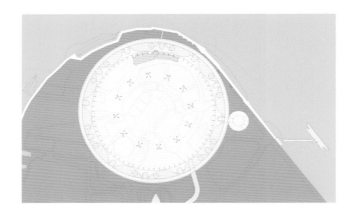

Site plan

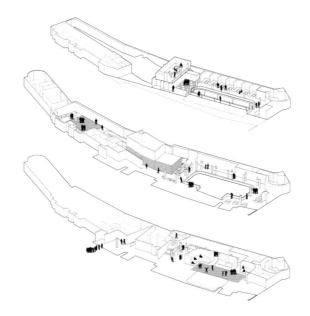

Axonometric

Belonging to the owners of the famous Fabric nightclub, Matter is a dance and live-music venue in the O2 Arena designed by Richard Rogers. The amenities cover three floors. The top two have balconies overlooking the main dance floor and the area set aside for concerts.

Die Diskothek Matter wurde von den Schöpfern der berühmten „Fabric" entworfen. Sie umfasst einen Raum für Live-Auftritte und erstreckt sich über drei Geschosse der von Richard Rogers geplanten O2 Arena. Aus den beiden oberen Stockwerken kann man von Balkonen auf die größte Tanzfläche und die Bühne sehen.

Des mêmes propriétaires de la célèbre discothèque « Fabric », Matter est une discothèque et une salle de concerts en direct qui se trouve dans O2 Arena, signée Richard Rogers. Les installations sont réparties sur trois étages. Les deux étages supérieurs ont des balcons donnant sur la piste de danse principale et la zone réservée aux concerts.

De eigenaren van het beroemde Fabric bezitten ook Matter, een discotheek en concertzaal voor livemuziek in de O2 arena, ontworpen door Richard Rogers. De diverse onderdelen zijn verdeeld over drie verdiepingen. De twee bovenste hebben balkons die uitkijken op de grote dansvloer en de concertzaal.

WORK

Cathedral (11)

9a St Thomas

Allford Hall Monaghan Morris
www.ahmm.co.uk

Photos: © Rob Parrish

Located in the old St Thomas's Church, the new offices of the Cathedral property group make the most of the building's special features in contrast with the contemporary decor. The space houses the Institution's art collection and facilitates access to the Old Operating Theatre Museum on the roof.

Das Immobilienunternehmen Cathedral richtete seine Büroräume in der ehemaligen St. Thomaskirche ein. Die besonderen Charakteristika des Bauwerkes stehen in lebhaftem Kontrast zur zeitgenössischen Ausstattung. Außer der Kunstsammlung des Unternehmens ist unter dem Dach des Gebäudes das Old Operating Theatre Museum untergebracht.

Situés dans l'ancienne église de St Thomas, les nouveaux bureaux du groupe immobilier Cathedral profitent des caractéristiques de la construction en contraste avec une décoration contemporaine. L'espace renferme la collection d'art de l'institution et permet d'accéder au Old Operating Theatre Museum sur le toit.

Het nieuwe kantoor van vastgoedgroep Cathedral in de voormalige St Thomas Church benut de bijzondere kenmerken van het gebouw die contrasteren met de moderne inrichting. De ruimte herbergt de kunstcollectie van de instelling en biedt toegang tot het Old Operating Theatre Museum in de dakruimte.

LEARN

Hatcham College (12)

Pepys Road

Jestico + Whiles
www.jesticowhiles.com

Photos: © Benedict Luxmore

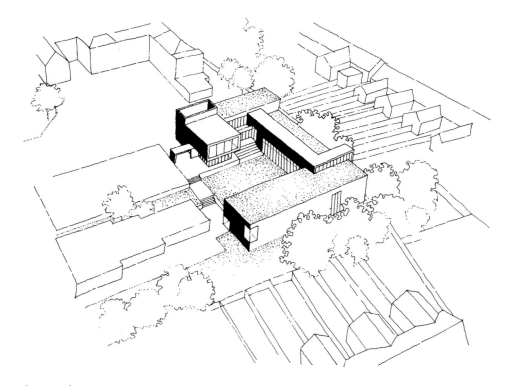

Axonometric

The design concept of this school is articulated in a succession of exterior spaces that define the campus perimeter and visually separate it from the neighboring buildings. Of note is a rectangular structure that projects over the courtyards.

Dieser Schulkomplex wurde so angelegt, dass eine Folge von Außenräumen entstanden ist, welche die Ausdehnung des Campus bestimmen und ihn gleichzeitig gegenüber der Umgebung abschirmen. Auffällig ist die schwebende rechteckige Struktur über einem der Höfe.

Le design de cette école s'articule autour d'une série d'espaces extérieurs marquant le périmètre du campus et le séparant visuellement du voisinage. Il dégage une structure rectangulaire en saillie sur l'une des cours.

Het ontwerp van deze school krijgt gestalte in een opeenvolging van buitenruimten die de omtrek van de campus aangeven en hem aan het oog van de omgeving onttrekken. De rechthoekige, uitstekende structuur boven een van de binnenplaatsen valt op.

HEAL

Heart of Hounslow Centre for Health 13

92 Bath Road

Penoyre & Prasad
www.penoyre-prasad.net

Photos: © Dennis Gilbert/VIEW; Steve Townsend CFA

Site plan

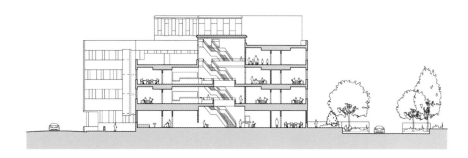

Section

The new building for this health and fitness center, one of the biggest in the UK, has a staggered shape and ranges from three to five stories along its length. The dark-gray cladding underlines the pastel tones of the aluminum and glass panels.

Dieses neue Gesundheitszentrum gehört zu den größten Großbritanniens. Es hat eine abgestufte Form mit drei bis fünf Geschossen. Durch die tiefgraue Verkleidung kommen die Pastelltöne der Glas- und Aluminiumpaneele besonders gut zur Geltung.

Le nouveau bâtiment de ce centre médical, l'un des plus grands du Royaume-Uni, a une forme décalée et s'élève sur trois à cinq étages. Le revêtement gris foncé rehausse les tons pastels des panneaux en aluminium et verre.

Dit nieuwe gezondheidscentrum, een van de grootste van het Verenigd Koninkrijk, heeft een trapsgewijze vorm die over de lengte drie tot vijf verdiepingen beslaat. Door de diepgrijze bekleding komen de pasteltinten van de aluminium en glazen panelen goed uit.

LEARN

Haberdashers's Aske's ⑭ Knights Academy

Launcelot Road

Jestico + Whiles
www.jesticowhiles.com

Photos: © Tim Crocker

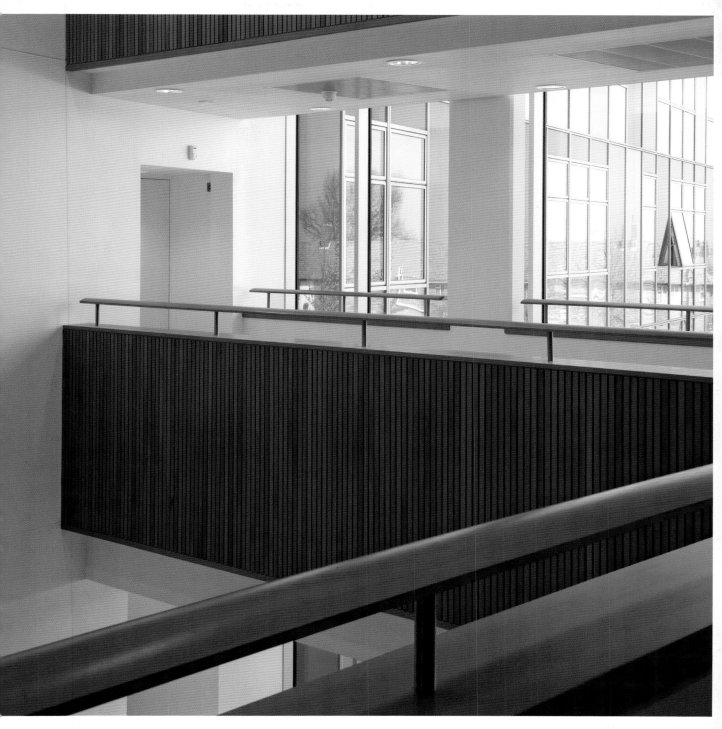

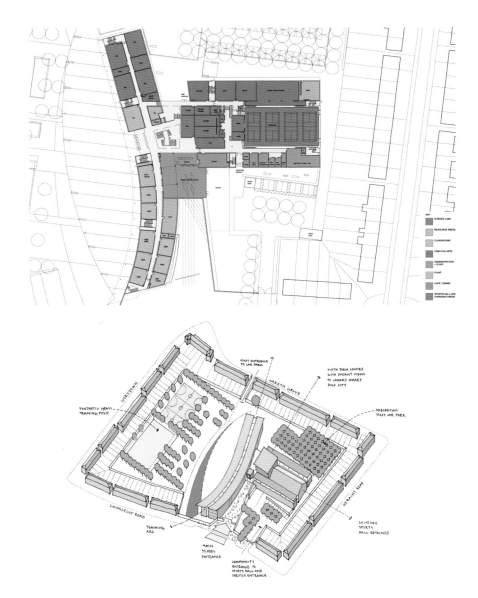

Floor plans

The new building for the teaching of sports science has a curved shape that ensures a better availability of outdoor space. Inside are the classrooms and common areas for exhibitions, informal meetings and social activities.

Die geschwungene Form des neuen Gebäudes für Sportwissenschaften gewährt eine bessere Nutzbarkeit der Außenanlagen. Im Inneren finden sich Lehrsäle sowie Räume für Ausstellungen, Besprechungen und andere gemeinschaftliche Aktivitäten.

Le nouveau bâtiment pour l'enseignement des sciences du sport possède une forme curviligne qui permet de mieux profiter de l'espace extérieur. L'intérieur compte les salles de cours et des espaces communs pour des expositions, des réunions informelles et des activités sociales.

Door de gebogen lijnen van het nieuwe gebouw voor sportwetenschappen is er meer buitenruimte beschikbaar. In het gebouw zijn collegezalen en ruimten voor tentoonstellingen, informele bijeenkomsten en sociale activiteiten ondergebracht.

LIVE

The Iroko Project 15

108 Stamford Street

Haworth Tompkins
www.haworthtompkins.com

Photos: © Edmund Sumner; Morley Von Sternberg; Helene Binet; Haworth Tompkins; Philip Vile

These buildings were raised on South Bank land which for years was home to industrial activity. After the works, the area was transformed into a block of 59 apartments with a large interior garden.

Auf einem Gelände der South Bank, das lange gewerblich genutzt wurde, entstanden diese Wohngebäude. Nach der Neugestaltung stehen den Nutzern nun 59 Wohnungen und ein großer begrünter Innenhof zur Verfügung.

Ces bâtiments ont été construits sur l'un des terrains de South Bank, longtemps lieu d'activité industrielle. Après l'intervention des architectes, la zone s'est convertie en un bloc de 59 appartements, avec un grand jardin intérieur.

Deze gebouwen kwamen op een stuk grond van de South Bank te staan, dat jarenlang een industrieterrein was. Na de architectonische ingreep veranderde het gebied in een blok van 59 appartementen met een grote binnentuin.

LIVE

Tooley Terrace ⑯

159-171 Tooley Street

Hawkins/Brown
www.hawkinsbrown.co.uk

Photos: © Tim Crocker

NEW
ROAD
LAYOUT

Elevation

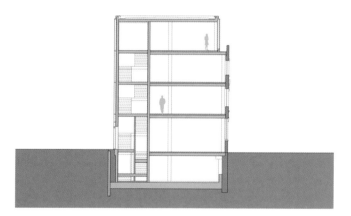

Section

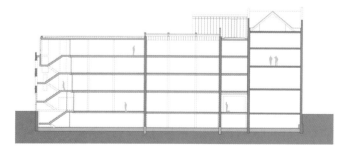

Section

This undertaking is the result of refitting works, the retention of the façade and new buildings. It houses small businesses and work spaces where before there was a group of practically abandoned buildings. The new façade elements maintain a rhythm in keeping with the existing ones in terms of shape and color.

Dieses Projekt entstand als Ergebnis der Umgestaltung mit Erhaltung der Fassade eines Altbaus und mehreren Neubauten. Wo sich früher nur verlassene Gebäude befanden, sind nun kleine Läden und Werkstätten untergebracht. Die neuen Fassaden wurden in Form und Farbe der alten angepasst und nehmen deren Rhythmus auf.

Ce chantier est le fruit de travaux portant sur le nouvel équipement, la conservation de la façade et la construction de nouveaux bâtiments. Il compte de petits commerces et des espaces de travail, là où se dressait avant un groupe d'immeubles quasiment à l'abandon. Les éléments nouveaux de la façade gardent un rythme cohérent en forme et couleur avec l'existant.

Dit bouwwerk kreeg bij zijn renovatie nieuwe voorzieningen; de gevel werd behouden en er kwam een nieuwe aanbouw. Waar voorheen enkele desolate gebouwen stonden, zijn nu kleine winkels en werkruimten ondergebracht. De nieuwe gevel-elementen gaan in vorm en kleur op in het ritme van de reeds bestaande.

LIVE

Neo Bankside 17

Sumner Street

Rogers Stirk Harbour + Partners
www.rsh-p.com

Drawings: © Rogers Stirk Harbour + Partners

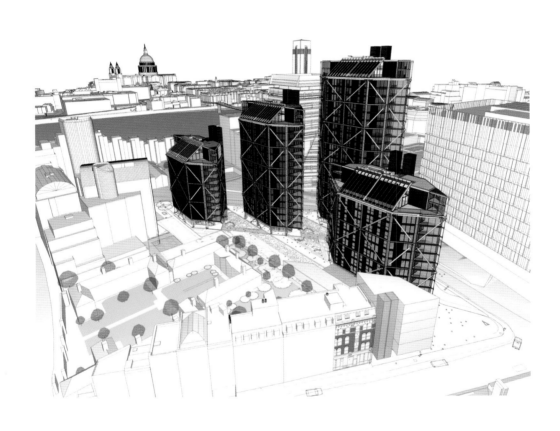

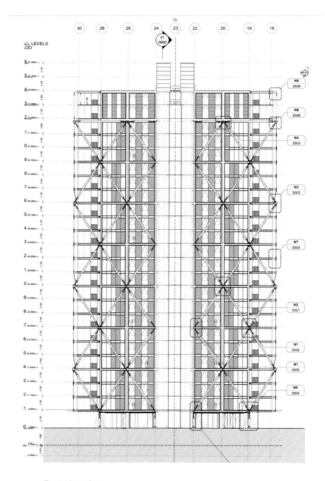

East elevation

This apartment complex will sit next to the Tate Modern and boast 197 apartments spread over four pavilions set in gardens. The blocks will vary in height from 9 to 24 stories.

Es ist vorgesehen, dass dieser Gebäudekomplex in unmittelbarer Nachbarschaft der Tate Modern Gallery in seinen vier Pavillons 197 Wohnungen aufnehmen wird. Die zwischen 9 und 24 Stockwerke umfassenden Pavillons sollen in einer Grünanlage stehen.

Cet ensemble de logements qui se dressera à côté de la galerie Tate Modern comptera 197 appartements répartis dans quatre pavillons entourés de jardins. La hauteur des blocs variera, de 9 à 24 étages.

Dit gebouwencomplex dat naast het Tate Modern komt te staan, zal 197 appartementen tellen die verdeeld zijn over vier door tuinen omringde paviljoens. De paviljoens zullen in hoogte verschillen: tussen de 9 en 24 verdiepingen.

LEARN

Clapham Manor Primary School ⑱

Belmont Road

dRMM/de Rijke Marsh Morgan Architects
www.drmm.co.uk

Photos: © Alex de Rijke; Jonas Lencer; Philip Mars

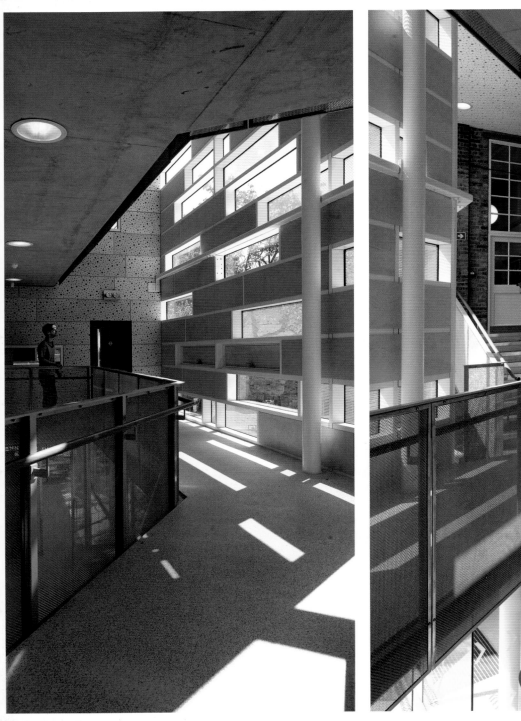

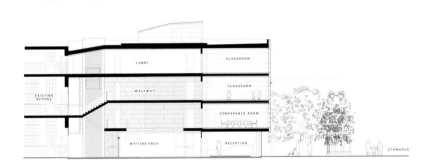

Section

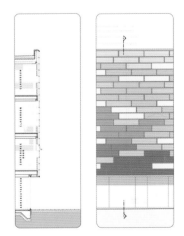

Section curtain wall

This addition to a 19th-century building has a façade inspired by the construction systems of post-War schools of architecture. As a result it features spaces with lots of natural light that are very well ventilated. The external appearance references a pixilated link that plays with the scale of the bricks of the neighboring buildings.

Der Entwurf für den Anbau eines Gebäudes aus dem 19. Jh. orientiert sich an den Fassaden der Schulgebäude der Nachkriegszeit. Entstanden sind so helle, gut durchlüftete Räume. Die Fassade wirkt wie ein Punktraster, das den Maßstab der Backsteinfassaden der Nachbargebäude spielerisch wieder aufnimmt.

Cette annexe à un bâtiment du XIXᵉ siècle affiche une façade inspirée des systèmes de construction des écoles d'après-guerre. Les espaces obtenus sont baignés de lumière naturelle et très bien ventilés. L'apparence extérieure renvoie à une trame originale qui joue avec la gamme des briques des bâtiments voisins.

Deze uitbouw van een 19e-eeuws gebouw heeft een gevel die is geïnspireerd op naoorlogse scholen. Hierdoor zijn goed geventileerde ruimten met veel daglicht ontstaan. De buitenkant herinnert aan een patroon van pixels dat speelt met de schaal van de bakstenen van de aangrenzende gebouwen.

CLASSICS

1 Natural History Museum

2 Royal Exchange

3 Royal Albert Hall

DOMINE·JESU·REX·ET·REDEMPTOR
PER·SANGUINEM·TUUM·SALVA·NOS

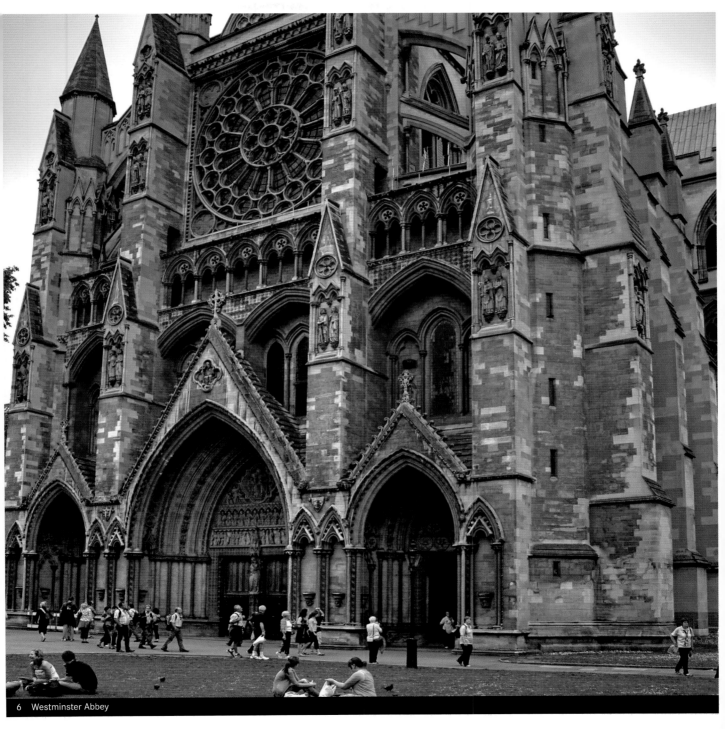

7   The National Gallery

8   Tower of London

DEFEND·THE·CHILDREN·OF·THE·
POOR·&·PVNISH·THE·WRONGDOER

11   Christ Church Spitalfields

12   St Martin in the Fields

14 Buckingham Palace

15 British Library

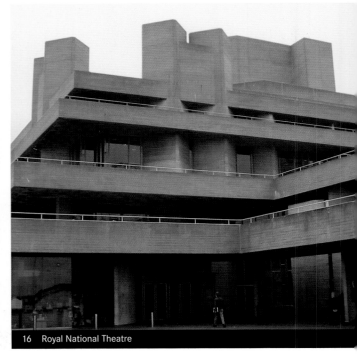

16 Royal National Theatre

18   Oxo Tower

19   BT Tower

20   Tate Modern Gallery

21   Reuters Building

22 Centre Point

23 42 Tower

26 London Eye

27 MoorHouse

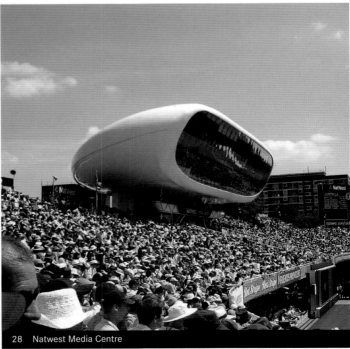

28 Natwest Media Centre

33   20 Bank Street

34   350 Euston Road

35   Bank of America

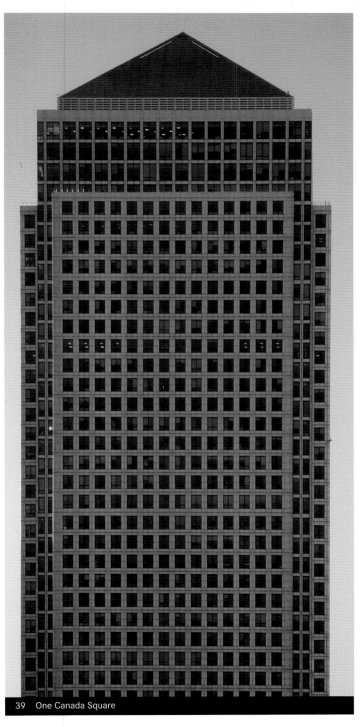

39   One Canada Square

40   One Churchill Place (Barclays Tower)

↑Way out   ↑DLR ⊖

42 Canada Square (HSBC Tower)

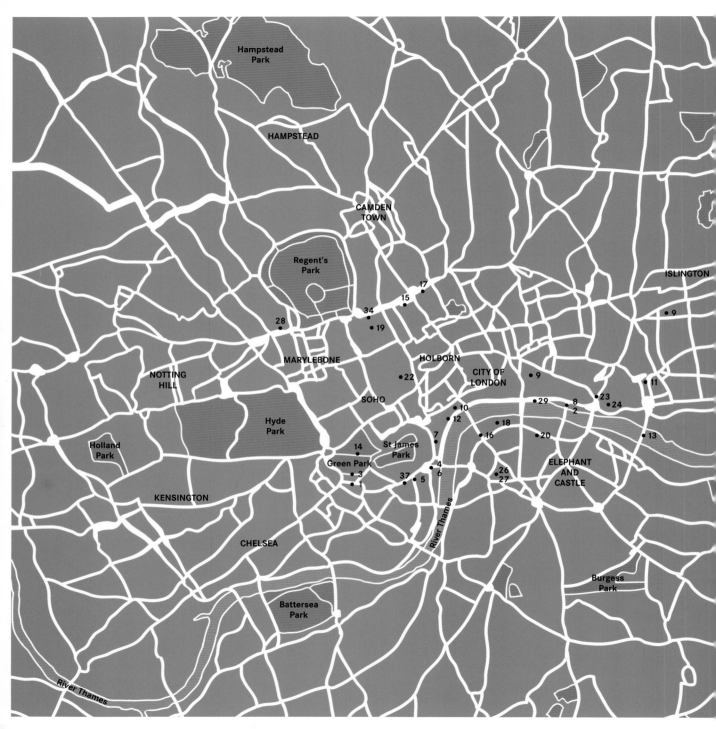

HACKNEY

Victoria
Park

STRATFORD

Wanstead
Flats Park

WEST HAM

STEPNEY

River Thames

ROTHERHITHE

21	● 38
31	39
32	40
33	41
35	42
36	43

●25

●30

River Thames

PECKHAM

NEW CROSS

GREENWICH

Greenwich
Park

Photo Credits